Flight was in his Spirit

The Life of Harry Burfield

September 10, 1915 - June 12, 1971

by Marion Ann Burfield

Library and Archives Canada Cataloguing in Publication

Burfield, Marion Ann
Flight was in his spirit : the life of Harry Burfield, September 10, 1915-June 12, 1971 / by Marion Ann Burfield.

Includes bibliographical references.
ISBN 978-1-927371-51-0

1. Burfield, Harry, 1915-1971. 2. Skiers--British Columbia--Biography. 3. Skis and skiing--British Columbia--History. 4. British Columbia--Biography. I. Title.

GV854.2.B87B87 2012 796.93'5092 C2012-901644-6

Published by RikKur Publishing
Printed in Canada by Friesens

Book design by Linda Parke Graphic Design
www.lindaparke.com

I would like to dedicate this book to my mother Katherine Ann Burfield, who stood beside my dad throughout his accomplishments, for her strength in trying to keep together Dad's dreams of a successful business. After the loss of not only her beloved husband Harry, but also her only son, Richard, she gave up hope of keeping the dreams alive. Until we lost her on June 17th 2006, she never loved again.

Also to my children, Riki Dawn Burfield and Kurt Stacy Burfield, for believing in my decision to bring to life a legacy of their grandfather, and their uncle Richard, who they never had the opportunity to meet.

Also to Glen C. Cox for standing beside me in my quest to bring this book to life.

Finally, I dedicate this book to all past, present, and future skiers of the world, for venturing out and who, like my dad and my brother, Richard, love the sport of skiing.

I would like to thank:

Fred and Peggy Burfield of Parksville, BC
The staff at the West Vancouver BC Archives
The staff at the Revelstoke BC Museum and Archives
The staff at the Nelson BC Museum and Archives
The North Shore News of North Vancouver, BC
Mayor Al Raine of Sun Peaks, BC
Sun Peaks Corporation
CFJC TV, Kamloops, BC
Linda Parke Graphic Design of Vancouver, BC
Barry Prost of the Camera House in Kamloops, BC
Mike Weigele of Blue River, BC
Rob White of Kamloops, BC
Reimer Bros Trucking of Armstrong, BC
Mary and Mike Dragani of Revelstoke, BC
The Kamloops Library
The Vancouver Sun and Province

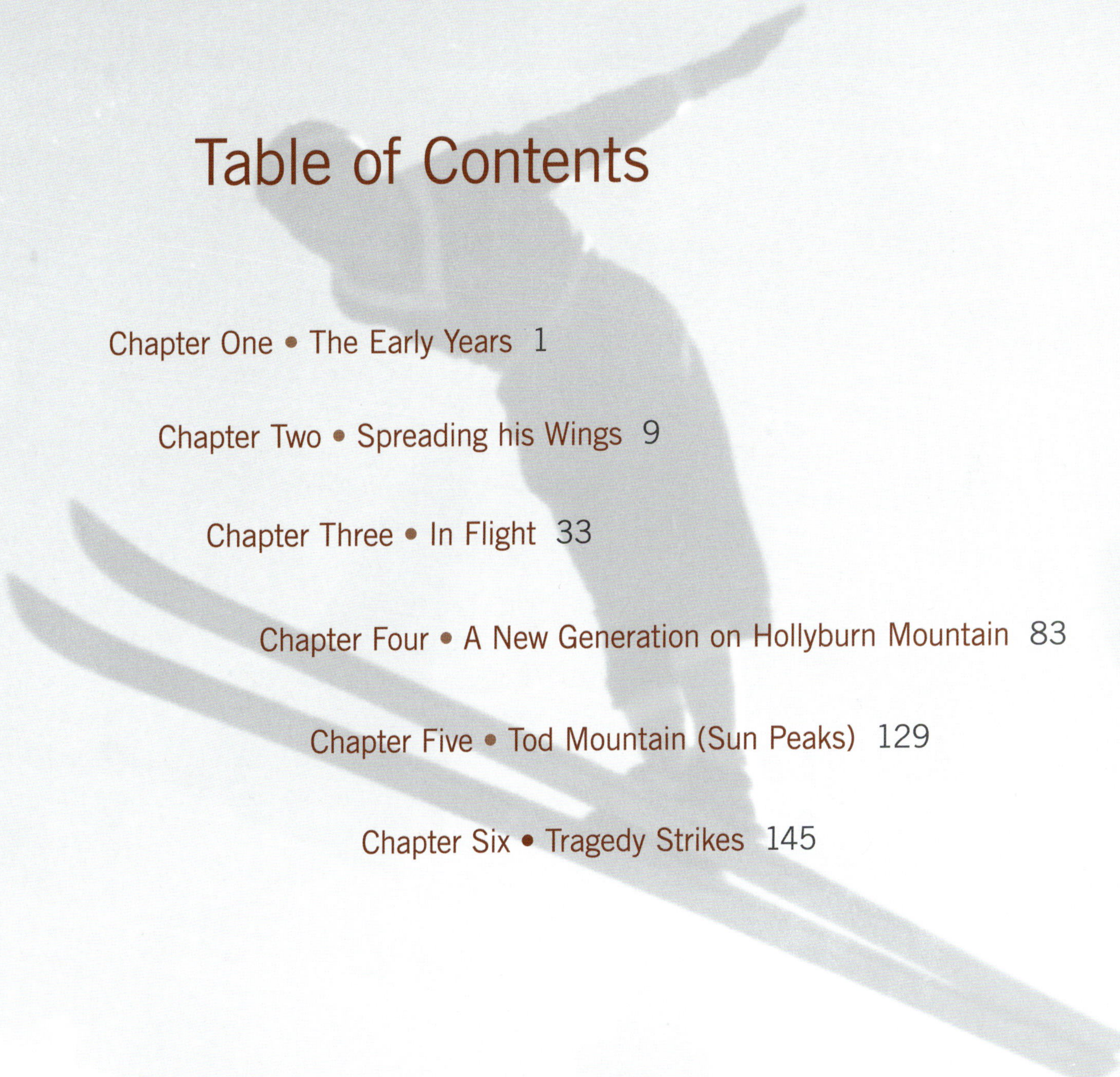

Table of Contents

Chapter One • The Early Years 1

Chapter Two • Spreading his Wings 9

Chapter Three • In Flight 33

Chapter Four • A New Generation on Hollyburn Mountain 83

Chapter Five • Tod Mountain (Sun Peaks) 129

Chapter Six • Tragedy Strikes 145

Thank you

My father, Harry Burfield, was one of many skiing pioneers in British Columbia, Canada. He had an immense passion for skiing and he loved to fly down the snowy slopes, through the air on two wooden boards. Jumping was all skiers did back in the 1920s and into the 30s. Groomed ski hills and rope tows were unheard of at the time. If Dad and his friends wanted to ski, they had to hike up the mountains. As the photographs show, they rarely wore jackets because they were working so hard.

Harry promoted the sport that he loved. Thanks to his efforts and the vision he shared with other prominent skiers of the day, millions of people today have the opportunity to enjoy skiing in British Columba.

— Marion Ann Burfield

Chapter One

The Early Years

George "Harry" Burfield was the first born to Joseph Harry and Emma Jane (Buckles) Burfield. He was born on September 10, 1915, in Revelstoke, British Columbia, Canada. He lived in Revelstoke for the first 10 years of his life with his younger brother Fred who was born June 21, 1918. They lived in a home known today as the Historic Taylor House from 1923 to 1931. Harry's father worked as an Express agent for CP Rail. During that time, in 1926, the family moved to England for two years, where Harry's father represented the Canadian fur trade and his mother worked as a fashion model.

In the early 1930s the family moved to Penticton, BC and later transferred to Nelson, BC. It was then that Harry, at a young age, discovered his passion for skiing.

facing page: Harry as an infant in Revelstoke, 1915.

Harry with his parents, Joseph Harry Burfield and Emma Jane (Buckles) Burfield, in Revelstoke, BC, 1915. Harry's father immigrated from England ca. 1912. His mother came soon after and they were married on July 10th, 1914 in Nelson BC. Harry's mother and father were very happy people and were always smiling. The Burfield family has a long legacy of good English humour.

Harry at age 3 in snowy Revelstoke, BC, 1918.

Harry's home in Revelstoke, ca. 1923-31, known today as the Historic Taylor House, lies kitty corner to the Revelstoke Court House. The home is now a designated Heritage Site.

Harry's brother Fred (left) and Harry (right) in the dining room of their home in Revelstoke. It seems from an early age there was something Harry liked about tall skies.

Marion Burfield took the heritage home tour of the Taylor House with local historian, Ruby Knobs, in 1992. When she entered the house, she felt as though she had stepped back in time. "It was nice to know that Dad had grown up in this great home."

PICTURE OF THE PAST

When the first mail plane was forced down in Revelstoke by a snowstorm on Oct. 14, 1920, many Revelstoke residents turned-out to look over the aircraft. Far left is Mr. Burfield, Sr., and Mrs. Burfield, second from right. The young boy could be the Burfield's son but he and the other three people in the photo were not identified. Mr. Burfield was the CP Express agent here for many years.

Far left is Mr. Burfield Sr., Harry's grandfather. Next to him is Joseph Burfield, Harry's father. Second from the right is Harry's mother. Harry is standing in the front. This clipping is from the Revelstoke newspaper.

Harry's grandparents immigrated from England after Harry's father and mother. Revelstoke's deep snow in 1919 didn't stop them from being photographed in formal dress!

H. BURFIELD DIES AT KAMLOOPS

Resided Here For Some Time With His Son

Mr. Harry Burfield, for some years a resident here with his son, Mr. J. H. Burfield, died at Kamloops Thursday afternoon, at the home of his daughter Mrs. H. J. Parker, at one time resident here.

Born in Lewes, Sussex, England, he had been a master builder and carpenter and came to this country about ten years ago. He was in his 81st year.

Mr. Burfield leaves to mourn him, his wife and daughter, and his son, J. H. Burfield, now at Nelson, where interment took place.

A man of interesting conversation, the late Mr. Burfield was a link with early Victorian times, and delighted in old stories, books and th[illegible] ly.

Harry's grandfather passed away in 1929.

Mrs. H. Burfield Dies at Kamloops

1936

Kamloops, Feb. 27.— There passed away early Monday morning Mrs. Ruth Burfield, relict of Harry Burfield, who died here in 1929. The deceased, who was the mother of Mrs. H. J. Parker, would have been 84 years of age on Wednesday. A son, J. H. Burfield, Westbay, West Vancouver, also survives.

Born in Framfield, Sussex, England, the late Mrs. Burfield came to Canada over 16 years ago and for the past eleven years had resided with Mr. and Mrs. Parker in Kamloops.

The funeral took place from Dwyer's Funeral Home on Wednesday afternoon, and Rev. W. F. Bushe conducted services at St. Paul's Cathedral Church at 2 o'clock. Interment was in Pleasant Street cemetery.

The late Mrs. Burfield was a resident with her late husband, in Revelstoke for a number of years, later living in Nelson before going to Kamloops.

Chapter Two

Spreading his Wings

Harry's skill progressed quickly during the 1930s, when he won many trophies, ribbons and pins for downhill racing and his favourite—ski jumping. He joined various competition classes and earned a reputation as a great ski competitor. He went up against many of the great skiers of the day including Nels Nelson, of Revelstoke, Bert and Bill Irwin of Princeton, Gus Johnson of Vancouver, and many other greats from around the world. Harry and other competitors traveled around British Columbia and the northwest United States to various ski hills, including many that don't exist today.

facing page: Harry with two of the many trophies he won.

One of the earliest photographs of Harry practising his jumping in Nelson, BC in the 1930s off a hand-made jump. There was a lot of shoveling to do to get the jump higher as his jumping ability progressed. In 1932 Harry was able to clear 90 feet and was hot on the heels of the pros who were jumping over 100 feet at the time. When Harry competed in Spokane, early in his career, as a member of the Nelson Amateur Ski Club in 1933 he came in 4th place.

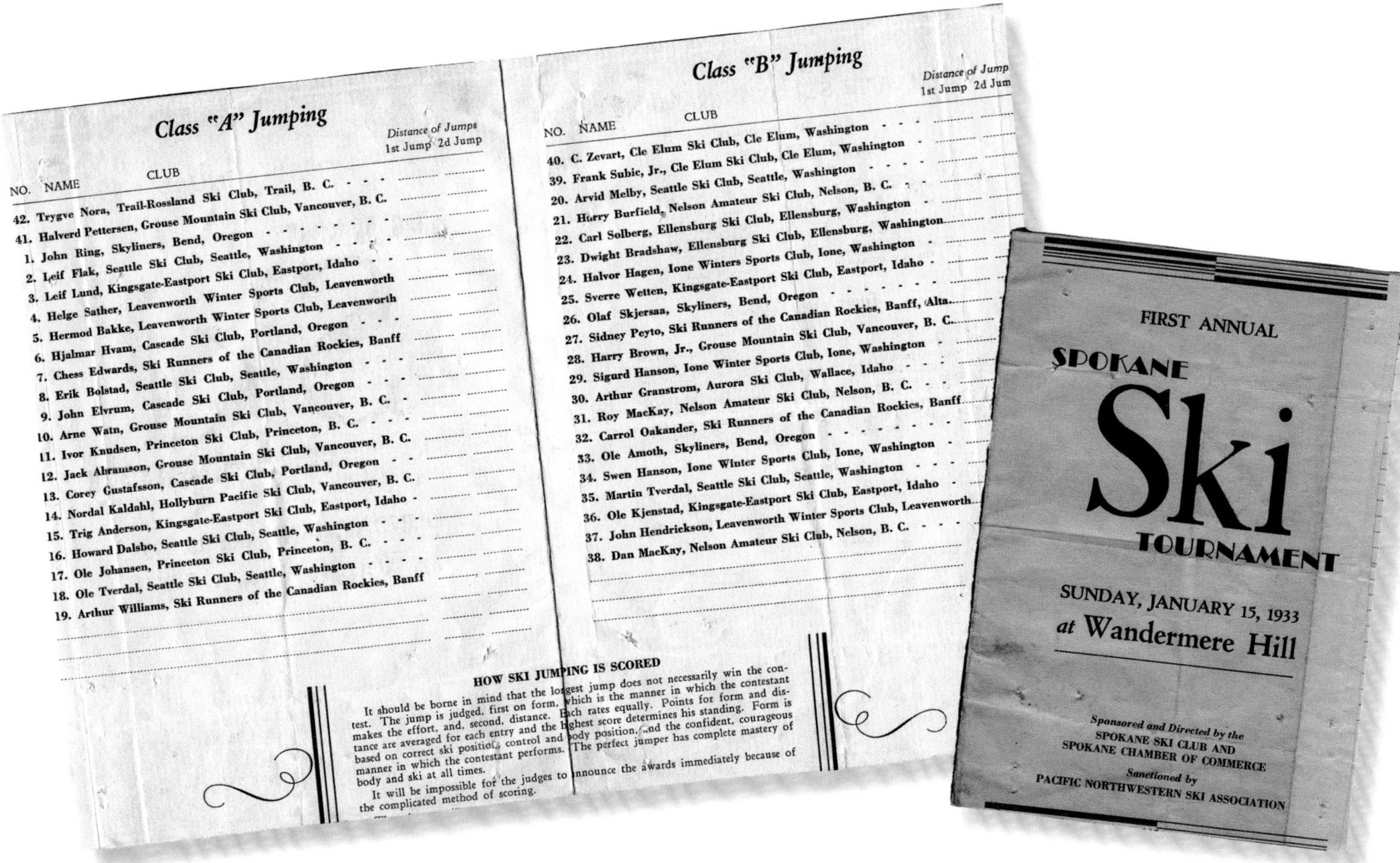

Class "A" Jumping

Distance of Jumps

NO.	NAME	CLUB	1st Jump	2d Jump
42.	Trygve Nora,	Trail-Rossland Ski Club, Trail, B. C.		
41.	Halverd Pettersen,	Grouse Mountain Ski Club, Vancouver, B. C.		
1.	John Ring,	Skyliners, Bend, Oregon		
2.	Leif Flak,	Seattle Ski Club, Seattle, Washington		
3.	Leif Lund,	Kingsgate-Eastport Ski Club, Eastport, Idaho		
4.	Helge Sather,	Leavenworth Winter Sports Club, Leavenworth		
5.	Hermod Bakke,	Leavenworth Winter Sports Club, Leavenworth		
6.	Hjalmar Hvam,	Cascade Ski Club, Portland, Oregon		
7.	Chess Edwards,	Ski Runners of the Canadian Rockies, Banff		
8.	Erik Bolstad,	Seattle Ski Club, Seattle, Washington		
9.	John Elvrum,	Cascade Ski Club, Portland, Oregon		
10.	Arne Watn,	Grouse Mountain Ski Club, Vancouver, B. C.		
11.	Ivor Knudsen,	Princeton Ski Club, Princeton, B. C.		
12.	Jack Abramson,	Grouse Mountain Ski Club, Portland, Oregon		
13.	Corey Gustafsson,	Cascade Ski Club, Portland, Oregon		
14.	Nordal Kaldahl,	Hollyburn Pacific Ski Club, Vancouver, B. C.		
15.	Trig Anderson,	Kingsgate-Eastport Ski Club, Eastport, Idaho		
16.	Howard Dalsbo,	Seattle Ski Club, Seattle, Washington		
17.	Ole Johansen,	Princeton Ski Club, Princeton, B. C.		
18.	Ole Tverdal,	Seattle Ski Club, Seattle, Washington		
19.	Arthur Williams,	Ski Runners of the Canadian Rockies, Banff		

Class "B" Jumping

Distance of Jump

NO.	NAME	CLUB	1st Jump	2d Jum
40.	C. Zevart,	Cle Elum Ski Club, Cle Elum, Washington		
39.	Frank Subic, Jr.,	Cle Elum Ski Club, Cle Elum, Washington		
20.	Arvid Melby,	Seattle Ski Club, Seattle, Washington		
21.	Harry Burfield,	Nelson Amateur Ski Club, Nelson, B. C.		
22.	Carl Solberg,	Ellensburg Ski Club, Ellensburg, Washington		
23.	Dwight Bradshaw,	Ellensburg Ski Club, Ellensburg, Washington		
24.	Halvor Hagen,	Ione Winters Sports Club, Ione, Washington		
25.	Sverre Wetten,	Kingsgate-Eastport Ski Club, Eastport, Idaho		
26.	Olaf Skjersaa,	Skyliners, Bend, Oregon		
27.	Sidney Peyto,	Ski Runners of the Canadian Rockies, Banff, Alta.		
28.	Harry Brown, Jr.,	Grouse Mountain Ski Club, Vancouver, B. C.		
29.	Sigurd Hanson,	Ione Winter Sports Club, Ione, Washington		
30.	Arthur Granstrom,	Aurora Ski Club, Wallace, Idaho		
31.	Roy MacKay,	Nelson Amateur Ski Club, Nelson, B. C.		
32.	Carrol Oakander,	Ski Runners of the Canadian Rockies, Banff		
33.	Ole Amoth,	Skyliners, Bend, Oregon		
34.	Swen Hanson,	Ione Winter Sports Club, Ione, Washington		
35.	Martin Tverdal,	Seattle Ski Club, Seattle, Washington		
36.	Ole Kjenstad,	Kingsgate-Eastport Ski Club, Eastport, Idaho		
37.	John Hendrickson,	Leavenworth Winter Sports Club, Leavenworth		
38.	Dan MacKay,	Nelson Amateur Ski Club, Nelson, B. C.		

HOW SKI JUMPING IS SCORED

It should be borne in mind that the longest jump does not necessarily win the contest. The jump is judged, first on form, which is the manner in which the contestant makes the effort, and, second, distance. Each rates equally. Points for form and distance are averaged for each entry and the highest score determines his standing. Form is based on correct ski position, control and body position, and the confident, courageous manner in which the contestant performs. The perfect jumper has complete mastery of body and ski at all times.

It will be impossible for the judges to announce the awards immediately because of the complicated method of scoring.

FIRST ANNUAL

SPOKANE

Ski

TOURNAMENT

SUNDAY, JANUARY 15, 1933

at Wandermere Hill

Sponsored and Directed by the
SPOKANE SKI CLUB AND
SPOKANE CHAMBER OF COMMERCE

Sanctioned by
PACIFIC NORTHWESTERN SKI ASSOCIATION

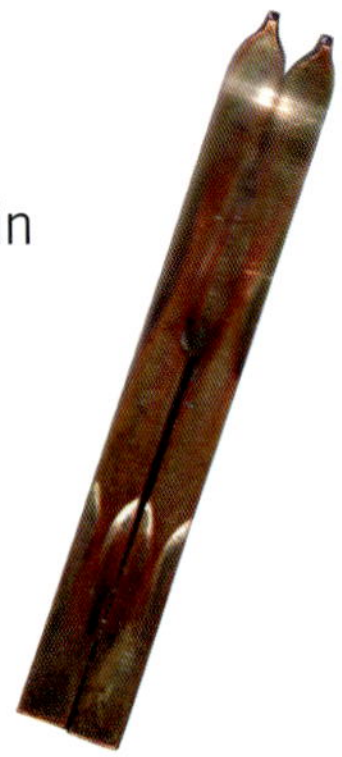

Brass ski pin

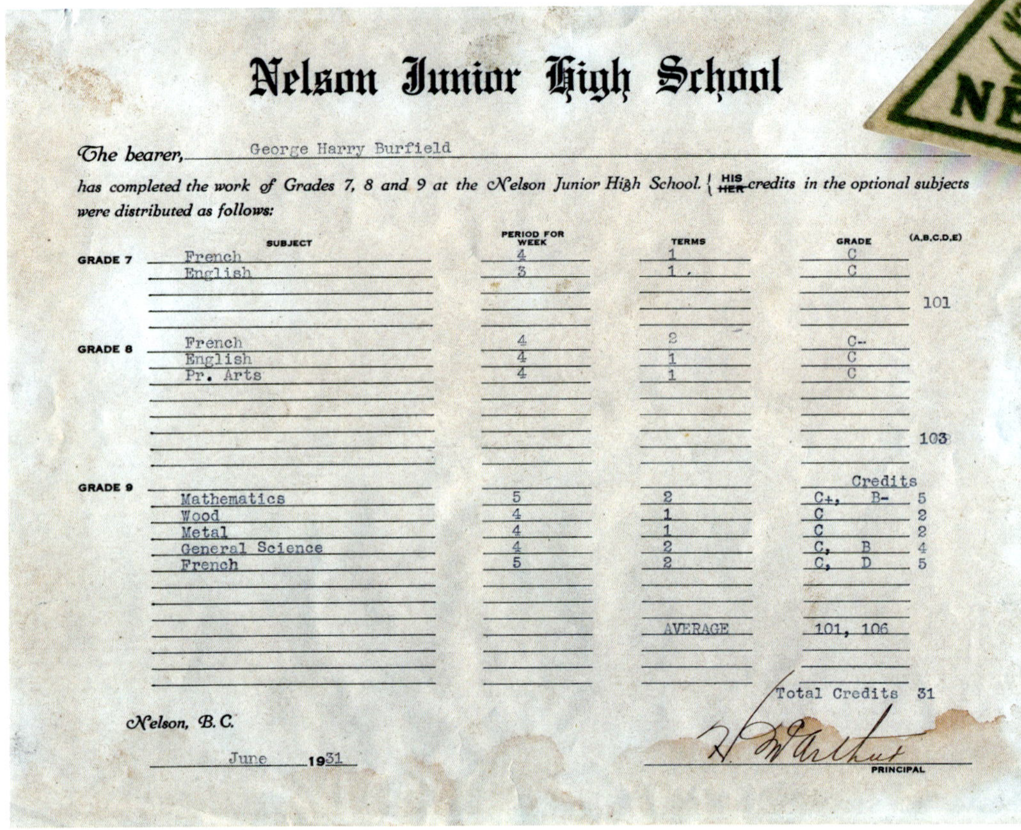

Nelson Junior High School

The bearer, George Harry Burfield

has completed the work of Grades 7, 8 and 9 at the Nelson Junior High School. { HIS ~~HER~~ *credits in the optional subjects were distributed as follows:*

	SUBJECT	PERIOD FOR WEEK	TERMS	GRADE	(A,B,C,D,E)
GRADE 7	French	4	1	C	
	English	3	1 .	C	
					101
GRADE 8	French	4	2	C-	
	English	4	1	C	
	Pr. Arts	4	1	C	
					103
				Credits	
GRADE 9	Mathematics	5	2	C+, B-	5
	Wood	4	1	C	2
	Metal	4	1	C	2
	General Science	4	2	C, B	4
	French	5	2	C, D	5
			AVERAGE	101, 106	
				Total Credits	31

Nelson, B.C.

June 1931

H. McArthur
PRINCIPAL

Harry's report card, June, 1931, shows that his grades were not as good as his ski jumping back in grades 7, 8 and 9. With a C average, we know where he spent most of his time!

If you look closely while driving east through Revelstoke, you can see the cut in the trees on the northeast face of the mountain, where the ski jumping hill used to be. The original wooden judge's tower rotted away long ago and a new metal tower was reconstructed in the early 60s. The park has plans to designate it a monument to symbolize the history of ski jumping in the area. Another popular ski jump was located near Hills, BC, south of Nakusp. Ski jumping was a thriving sport in the thirties and forties, until the start of the Second World War. After the war the skiers came back and continued jumping at the Revelstoke hill until the early 60s when the Trans Canada highway was relocated from the Big Bend highway and the ski hill was relocated to its current location.

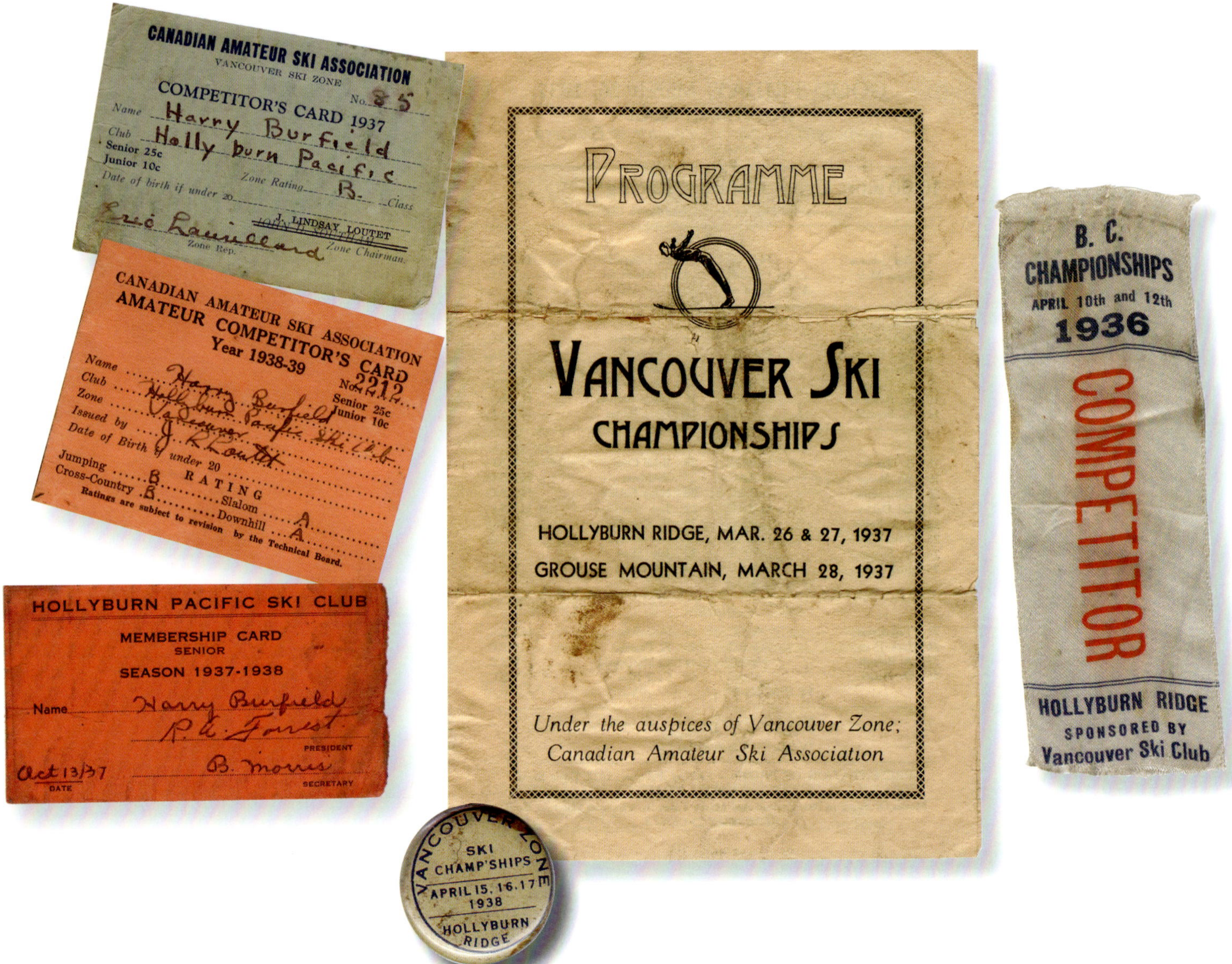
CANADIAN AMATEUR SKI ASSOCIATION
VANCOUVER SKI ZONE
COMPETITOR'S CARD 1937
No. 85
Name Harry Burfield
Club Hollyburn Pacific
Senior 25c
Junior 10c
Date of birth if under 20
Zone Rating B.
Class
J. LINDSAY LOUTET
Zone Rep.
Zone Chairman
CANADIAN AMATEUR SKI ASSOCIATION
AMATEUR COMPETITOR'S CARD
Year 1938-39
No. 2212
Senior 25c
Junior 10c
Name Harry Burfield
Club
Zone
Issued by
Date of Birth if under 20
RATING
Jumping B
Cross-Country B
Slalom A
Downhill A
Ratings are subject to revision by the Technical Board.
HOLLYBURN PACIFIC SKI CLUB
MEMBERSHIP CARD
SENIOR
SEASON 1937-1938
Name Harry Burfield
PRESIDENT
Oct 13/37
DATE
SECRETARY
PROGRAMME
VANCOUVER SKI
CHAMPIONSHIPS
HOLLYBURN RIDGE, MAR. 26 & 27, 1937
GROUSE MOUNTAIN, MARCH 28, 1937
Under the auspices of Vancouver Zone;
Canadian Amateur Ski Association
VANCOUVER ZONE
SKI
CHAMP'SHIPS
APRIL 15. 16. 17
1938
HOLLYBURN
RIDGE
B. C.
CHAMPIONSHIPS
APRIL 10th and 12th
1936
COMPETITOR
HOLLYBURN RIDGE
SPONSORED BY
Vancouver Ski Club

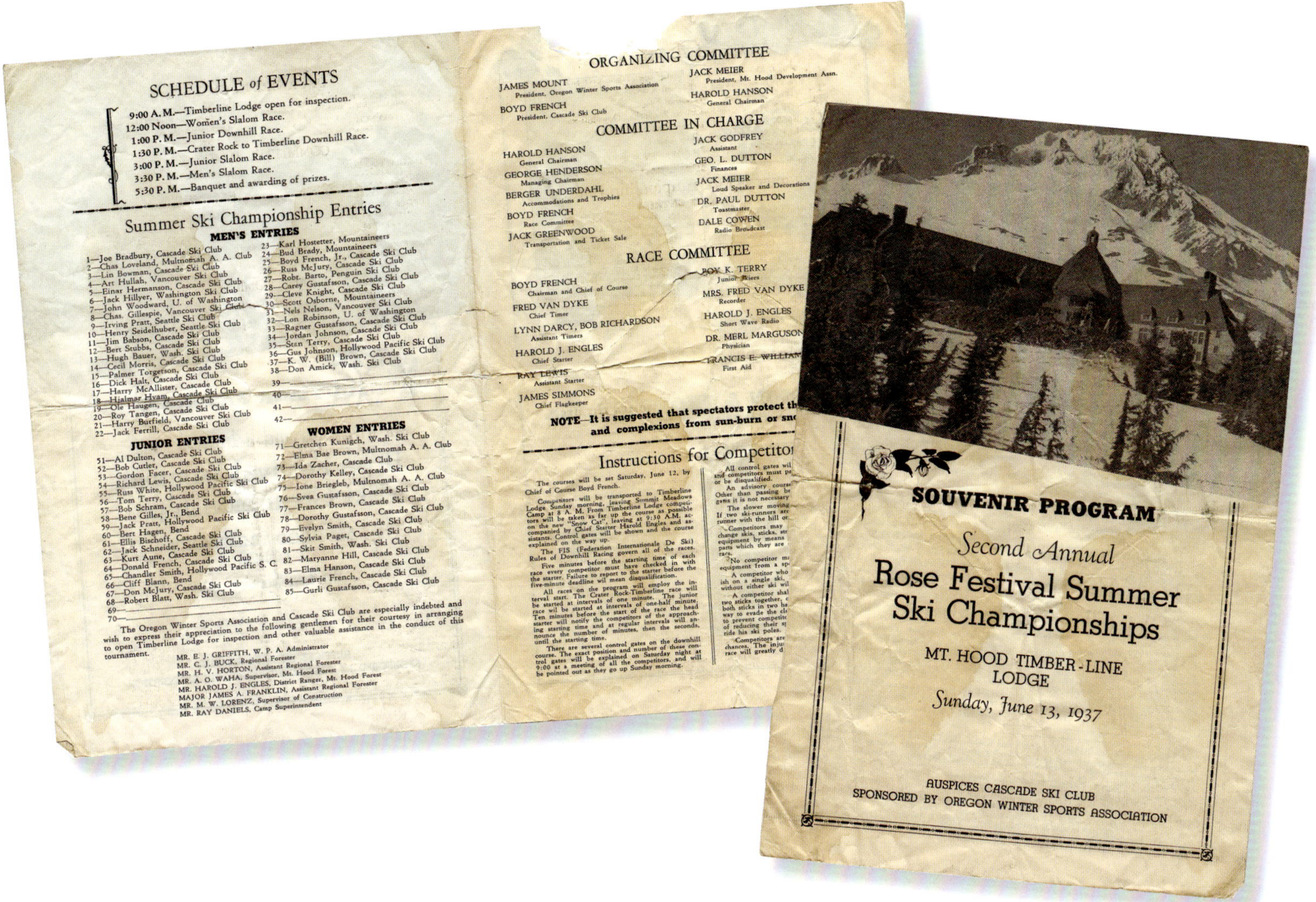

SCHEDULE *of* EVENTS

9:00 A. M.—Timberline Lodge open for inspection.
12:00 Noon—Women's Slalom Race.
1:00 P. M.—Junior Downhill Race.
1:30 P. M.—Crater Rock to Timberline Downhill Race.
3:00 P. M.—Junior Slalom Race.
3:30 P. M.—Men's Slalom Race.
5:30 P. M.—Banquet and awarding of prizes.

Summer Ski Championship Entries

MEN'S ENTRIES

1—Joe Bradbury, Cascade Ski Club
2—Chas Loveland, Multnomah A. A. Club
3—Lin Bowman, Cascade Ski Club
4—Art Hullah, Vancouver Ski Club
5—Einar Hermanson, Cascade Ski Club
6—Jack Hillyer, Washington Ski Club
7—John Woodward, U. of Washington
8—Chas. Gillespie, Vancouver Ski Club
9—Irving Pratt, Seattle Ski Club
10—Henry Seidelhuber, Seattle Ski Club
11—Jim Babson, Cascade Ski Club
12—Bert Stubbs, Cascade Ski Club
13—Hugh Bauer, Wash. Ski Club
14—Cecil Morris, Cascade Ski Club
15—Palmer Torgetson, Cascade Ski Club
16—Dick Halt, Cascade Ski Club
17—Harry McAllister, Cascade Club
18—Hjalmar Hvam, Cascade Ski Club
19—Ole Haugen, Cascade Club
20—Roy Tangen, Cascade Ski Club
21—Harry Burfield, Vancouver Ski Club
22—Jack Ferrill, Cascade Ski Club
23—Karl Hostetter, Mountaineers
24—Bud Brady, Mountaineers
25—Boyd French, Jr., Cascade Ski Club
26—Russ McJury, Cascade Ski Club
27—Robt. Barto, Penguin Ski Club
28—Carey Gustafsson, Cascade Ski Club
29—Cleve Knight, Cascade Ski Club
30—Scott Osborne, Mountaineers
31—Nels Nelson, Vancouver Ski Club
32—Lon Robinson, U. of Washington
33—Ragner Gustafsson, Cascade Ski Club
34—Jordan Johnson, Cascade Ski Club
35—Stan Terry, Cascade Ski Club
36—Gus Johnson, Hollywood Pacific Ski Club
37—K. W. (Bill) Brown, Cascade Ski Club
38—Don Amick, Wash. Ski Club
39—
40—
41—
42—

JUNIOR ENTRIES

51—Al Dulton, Cascade Ski Club
52—Bob Cutler, Cascade Ski Club
53—Gordon Facer, Cascade Ski Club
54—Richard Lewis, Cascade Ski Club
55—Russ White, Hollywood Pacific Ski Club
56—Tom Terry, Cascade Ski Club
57—Bob Schram, Cascade Ski Club
58—Bene Gilles, Jr., Bend
59—Jack Pratt, Hollywood Pacific Ski Club
60—Bert Hagen, Bend
61—Ellis Bischoff, Cascade Ski Club
62—Jack Schneider, Seattle Ski Club
63—Kurt Aune, Cascade Ski Club
64—Donald French, Cascade Ski Club
65—Chandler Smith, Hollywood Pacific S. C.
66—Cliff Blann, Bend
67—Don McJury, Cascade Ski Club
68—Robert Blatt, Wash. Ski Club
69—
70—

WOMEN ENTRIES

71—Gretchen Kunigch, Wash. Ski Club
72—Elma Bae Brown, Multnomah A. A. Club
73—Ida Zacher, Cascade Club
74—Dorothy Kelley, Cascade Ski Club
75—Ione Briegleb, Multnomah A. A. Club
76—Svea Gustafsson, Cascade Ski Club
77—Frances Brown, Cascade Ski Club
78—Dorothy Gustafsson, Cascade Ski Club
79—Evelyn Smith, Cascade Ski Club
80—Sylvia Paget, Cascade Ski Club
81—Skit Smith, Wash. Ski Club
82—Maryanne Hill, Cascade Ski Club
83—Elma Hanson, Cascade Ski Club
84—Laurie French, Cascade Ski Club
85—Gurli Gustafsson, Cascade Ski Club

The Oregon Winter Sports Association and Cascade Ski Club are especially indebted and wish to express their appreciation to the following gentlemen for their courtesy in arranging to open Timberline Lodge for inspection and other valuable assistance in the conduct of this tournament.

MR. E. J. GRIFFITH, W. P. A. Administrator
MR. C. J. BUCK, Regional Forester
MR. H. V. HORTON, Assistant Regional Forester
MR. A. O. WAHA, Supervisor, Mt. Hood Forest
MR. HAROLD J. ENGLES, District Ranger, Mt. Hood Forest
MAJOR JAMES A. FRANKLIN, Assistant Regional Forester
MR. M. W. LORENZ, Supervisor of Construction
MR. RAY DANIELS, Camp Superintendent

ORGANIZING COMMITTEE

JAMES MOUNT
President, Oregon Winter Sports Association

BOYD FRENCH
President, Cascade Ski Club

JACK MEIER
President, Mt. Hood Development Assn.

HAROLD HANSON
General Chairman

COMMITTEE IN CHARGE

HAROLD HANSON
General Chairman

GEORGE HENDERSON
Managing Chairman

BERGER UNDERDAHL
Accommodations and Trophies

BOYD FRENCH
Race Committee

JACK GREENWOOD
Transportation and Ticket Sale

JACK GODFREY
Assistant

GEO. L. DUTTON
Finances

JACK MEIER
Loud Speaker and Decorations

DR. PAUL DUTTON
Toastmaster

DALE COWEN
Radio Broadcast

RACE COMMITTEE

BOYD FRENCH
Chairman and Chief of Course

FRED VAN DYKE
Chief Timer

LYNN DARCY, BOB RICHARDSON
Assistant Timers

HAROLD J. ENGLES
Chief Starter

RAY LEWIS
Assistant Starter

JAMES SIMMONS
Chief Flagkeeper

ROY K. TERRY
Junior Skiers

MRS. FRED VAN DYKE
Recorder

HAROLD J. ENGLES
Short Wave Radio

DR. MERL MARGUSON
Physician

FRANCIS E. WILLIAM
First Aid

NOTE—It is suggested that spectators protect th
and complexions from sun-burn or sn

Instructions for Competito

The courses will be set Saturday, June 12, by Chief of Course Boyd French.

Competitors will be transported to Timberline Lodge Sunday morning, leaving Summit Meadows Camp at 8 A. M. From Timberline Lodge competitors will be taken as far up the course as possible on the new "Snow Cat", leaving at 9:30 A.M. accompanied by Chief Starter Harold Engles and assistants. Control gates will be shown and the course explained on the way up.

The FIS (Federation Internationale De Ski) Rules of Downhill Racing govern all of the races.

Five minutes before the starting time of each race every competitor must have checked in with the starter. Failure to report to the starter before the five-minute deadline wil mean disqualification.

All races on the program will employ the interval start. The Crater Rock-Timberline race will be started at intervals of one minute. The junior race wil be started at intervals of one-half minute. Ten minutes before the start of the race the head starter will notify the competitors of the approaching starting time and at regular intervals will announce the number of minutes, then the seconds, until the starting time.

There are several control gates on the downhill course. The exact position and number of these control gates will be explained on Saturday night at 9:00 at a meeting of all the competitors, and will be pointed out as they go up Sunday morning.

All control gates wil
and competitors must pa
or be disqualified.

An advisory course
Other than passing be
gates it is not necessary

The slower moving
If two ski-runners are
runner with the hill or

Competitors may
change skis, sticks, str
equipment by means
parts which they are
race.

No competitor ma
equipment from a sp

A competitor who
ish on a single ski,
without either ski wil

A competitor shal
two sticks together, c
both sticks in two ha
way to evade the cl
to prevent competit
of reducing their sp
ride his ski poles.

Competitors are
chances. The inju
race will greatly d

SOUVENIR PROGRAM

Second Annual

Rose Festival Summer Ski Championships

MT. HOOD TIMBER-LINE LODGE

Sunday, June 13, 1937

AUSPICES CASCADE SKI CLUB
SPONSORED BY OREGON WINTER SPORTS ASSOCIATION

SKI CARNIVAL IS BIG SUCCESS

(Continued from page one.)

The first inkling that spectators had of how successful the affair would be came before they left downtown Spokane. As the cars swung into Division street on the way out they fell into a solid line headed toward Wandermere and gradually this became a double and then a triple line.

As an illustration of what the drivers were up against the experience of the official party is a good illustration. King Boreas and Queen Aurora, with their retinue, left the Davenport hotel at 12:35 o'clock to make the nine-mile run and open the exercises at 1:30 o'clock. Mayor Funk was in the first car with the king and queen and little difficulty was expected.

Party Is Halted.

By the time the party reached the city line it was hedged in in a double line of cars and soon after this became a triple line. When 1:30 came the party was still a mile from the grounds, at a standstill, and it was 1:50 when it reached the special platform that had been set aside for its use.

This necessitated cutting the opening exercises to the bone, the half hour program being condensed into 10 minutes. Queen Aurora (Miss Margaret Bement) gave her welcome to the crowd and King Boreas (Eric Johnson) issued his proclamation. Mayor Funk was introduced and simply waved his hand, foregoing any talk at all. Then the American and British flags were hoisted and the stage was set.

Unique Stage Setting.

It was a unique stage setting for a ski jump. In the middle was the stretch of snow composing the hill, a ribbon 30 feet wide at the middle and gradually opening out to 60 feet at the bottom with the landing field running out 100 yards and ending in a huge pile of straw.

Halfway up, where the take-off was, were two stands on either side, one for the judges and the other for the newspaper men and photographers. Above that was the narrow runway stretching above for another 100 yards.

Crowd Lines Hill.

Lined along both sides of the hill, behind ropes, was the crowd, at least that part of it that elected to watch the fun on foot. It stretched from the very end of the landing field to the take-off, two solid ranks five or six deep and scattered out so that there was little idea of the number present.

In back of the end of the landing stage, parked all over the golf course in row after row, were literally hundreds of automobiles and in many cases their occupants chose to watch the fun from the comfort of glass-enclosed seats rather than face the chilling wind outside.

Crowd Is Amusing.

The crowd itself was interesting and amusing, particularly in the way it dressed to meet the winter conditions. One girl strolled along with a most becoming ski suit, warm and suitable for the day, but her feet enclosed in satin high heel shoes, thin-soled and bare of any other protection against the cold ground.

At least two women, mindful of the dictates of fashion, sported new spring straw hats, others wore riding clothes and boots. Ski clothes of the latest styles and fur coats, however, predominated.

First Jumper Down.

But let's get back to the meet. As the final notes of the bugles died away after the flag-raising a whistle blew and the trumpets sounded "Attention!" A red flag waved and, with a shout from the crowd of "Here he comes!" C. Zevart of the Cle Elum Ski club, shot down the course and launched himself into space, the first of the jumpers to make the trip.

The class B men led off and they followed each other in rapid succession. The first two landed and made the trip to the bottom without trouble, but the next two fell as they landed and wound up in a tangled mass of skis, head first, almost at the bottom of the hill. Neither one was hurt, but it gave the crowd its first big thrill and a chance to gasp.

Ambulance on Hand.

This is to Certify that

Name Harry Burfield

Address Vancouver B.C.

Club H.P.S.C. CASA Amateur Card No.

is a member of the Canadian Amateur Ski Association and an Amateur under the CASA and FIS Rules and is hereby granted permission to enter for the international events stated on this permit during the season of 1938.

Date Apr. 5/38

Signature E. Lauillard

Office Competitors' Committee

EVENTS

Mt Baker April 10th, 1938

Competitor's International Permit

CANADIAN AMATEUR SKI ASSOCIATION

In order to compete in all skiing events, Harry had to be a member of the Canadian Amateur Ski Association.

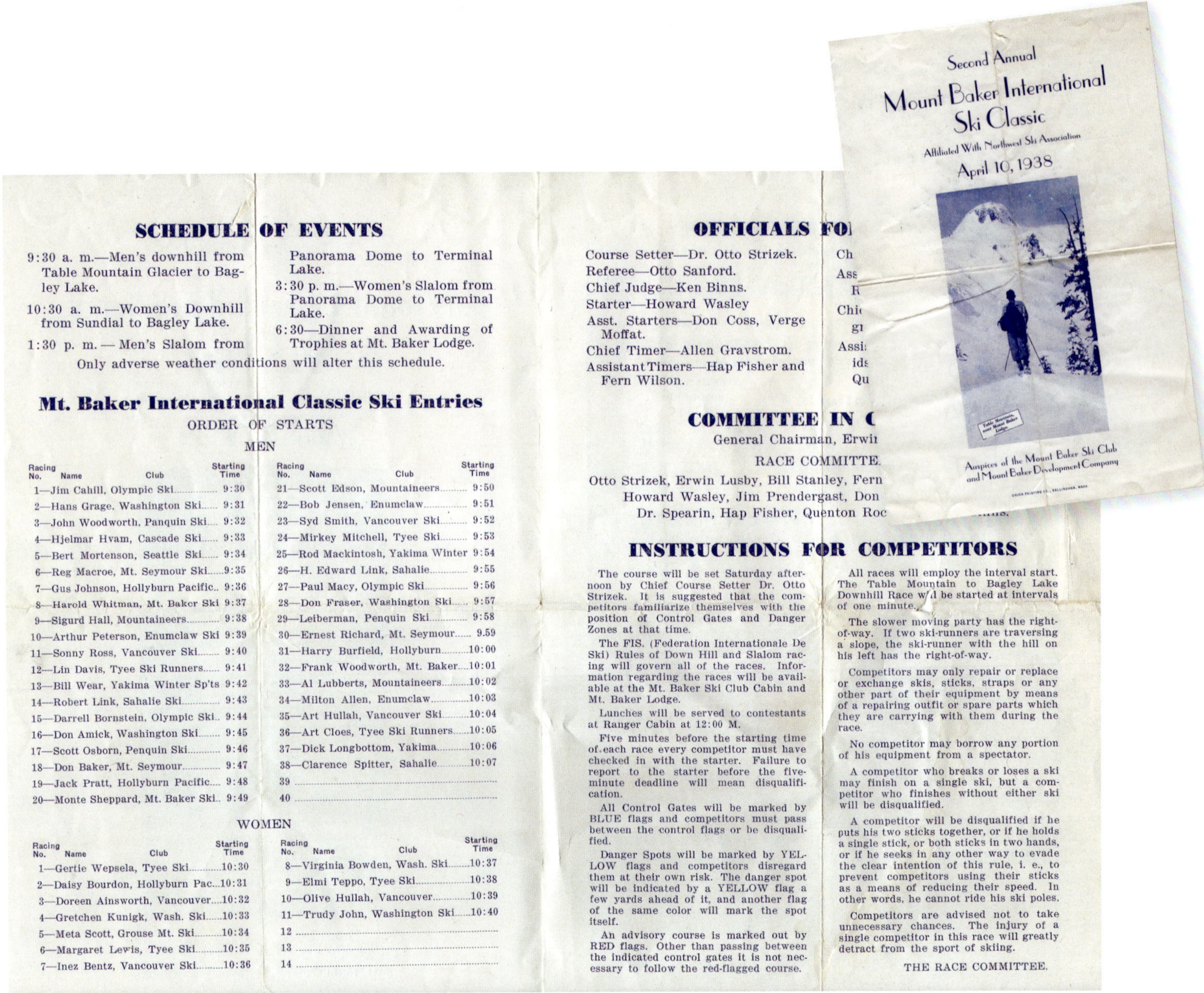

Second Annual

Mount Baker International Ski Classic

Affiliated With Northwest Ski Association

April 10, 1938

Table Mountain, near Mount Baker Lodge.

Auspices of the Mount Baker Ski Club and Mount Baker Development Company

UNION PRINTING CO., BELLINGHAM, WASH.

SCHEDULE OF EVENTS

9:30 a. m.—Men's downhill from Table Mountain Glacier to Bagley Lake.

10:30 a. m.—Women's Downhill from Sundial to Bagley Lake.

1:30 p. m. — Men's Slalom from Panorama Dome to Terminal Lake.

3:30 p. m.—Women's Slalom from Panorama Dome to Terminal Lake.

6:30—Dinner and Awarding of Trophies at Mt. Baker Lodge.

Only adverse weather conditions will alter this schedule.

Mt. Baker International Classic Ski Entries

ORDER OF STARTS

MEN

Racing No.	Name	Club	Starting Time
1	Jim Cahill	Olympic Ski	9:30
2	Hans Grage	Washington Ski	9:31
3	John Woodworth	Panquin Ski	9:32
4	Hjelmar Hvam	Cascade Ski	9:33
5	Bert Mortenson	Seattle Ski	9:34
6	Reg Macroe	Mt. Seymour Ski	9:35
7	Gus Johnson	Hollyburn Pacific	9:36
8	Harold Whitman	Mt. Baker Ski	9:37
9	Sigurd Hall	Mountaineers	9:38
10	Arthur Peterson	Enumclaw Ski	9:39
11	Sonny Ross	Vancouver Ski	9:40
12	Lin Davis	Tyee Ski Runners	9:41
13	Bill Wear	Yakima Winter Sp'ts	9:42
14	Robert Link	Sahalie Ski	9:43
15	Darrell Bornstein	Olympic Ski	9:44
16	Don Amick	Washington Ski	9:45
17	Scott Osborn	Penquin Ski	9:46
18	Don Baker	Mt. Seymour	9:47
19	Jack Pratt	Hollyburn Pacific	9:48
20	Monte Sheppard	Mt. Baker Ski	9:49
21	Scott Edson	Mountaineers	9:50
22	Bob Jensen	Enumclaw	9:51
23	Syd Smith	Vancouver Ski	9:52
24	Mirkey Mitchell	Tyee Ski	9:53
25	Rod Mackintosh	Yakima Winter	9:54
26	H. Edward Link	Sahalie	9:55
27	Paul Macy	Olympic Ski	9:56
28	Don Fraser	Washington Ski	9:57
29	Leiberman	Penquin Ski	9:58
30	Ernest Richard	Mt. Seymour	9.59
31	Harry Burfield	Hollyburn	10:00
32	Frank Woodworth	Mt. Baker	10:01
33	Al Lubberts	Mountaineers	10:02
34	Milton Allen	Enumclaw	10:03
35	Art Hullah	Vancouver Ski	10:04
36	Art Cloes	Tyee Ski Runners	10:05
37	Dick Longbottom	Yakima	10:06
38	Clarence Spitter	Sahalie	10:07
39			
40			

WOMEN

Racing No.	Name	Club	Starting Time
1	Gertie Wepsela	Tyee Ski	10:30
2	Daisy Bourdon	Hollyburn Pac.	10:31
3	Doreen Ainsworth	Vancouver	10:32
4	Gretchen Kunigk	Wash. Ski	10:33
5	Meta Scott	Grouse Mt. Ski	10:34
6	Margaret Lewis	Tyee Ski	10:35
7	Inez Bentz	Vancouver Ski	10:36
8	Virginia Bowden	Wash. Ski	10:37
9	Elmi Teppo	Tyee Ski	10:38
10	Olive Hullah	Vancouver	10:39
11	Trudy John	Washington Ski	10:40
12			
13			
14			

OFFICIALS FO

Course Setter—Dr. Otto Strizek.
Referee—Otto Sanford.
Chief Judge—Ken Binns.
Starter—Howard Wasley
Asst. Starters—Don Coss, Verge Moffat.
Chief Timer—Allen Gravstrom.
Assistant Timers—Hap Fisher and Fern Wilson.

COMMITTEE IN C

General Chairman, Erwi

RACE COMMITTE

Otto Strizek, Erwin Lusby, Bill Stanley, Fern
Howard Wasley, Jim Prendergast, Don
Dr. Spearin, Hap Fisher, Quenton Roc

INSTRUCTIONS FOR COMPETITORS

The course will be set Saturday afternoon by Chief Course Setter Dr. Otto Strizek. It is suggested that the competitors familiarize themselves with the position of Control Gates and Danger Zones at that time.

The FIS. (Federation Internationale De Ski) Rules of Down Hill and Slalom racing will govern all of the races. Information regarding the races will be available at the Mt. Baker Ski Club Cabin and Mt. Baker Lodge.

Lunches will be served to contestants at Ranger Cabin at 12:00 M.

Five minutes before the starting time of each race every competitor must have checked in with the starter. Failure to report to the starter before the five-minute deadline will mean disqualification.

All Control Gates will be marked by BLUE flags and competitors must pass between the control flags or be disqualified.

Danger Spots will be marked by YELLOW flags and competitors disregard them at their own risk. The danger spot will be indicated by a YELLOW flag a few yards ahead of it, and another flag of the same color will mark the spot itself.

An advisory course is marked out by RED flags. Other than passing between the indicated control gates it is not necessary to follow the red-flagged course.

All races will employ the interval start. The Table Mountain to Bagley Lake Downhill Race will be started at intervals of one minute.

The slower moving party has the right-of-way. If two ski-runners are traversing a slope, the ski-runner with the hill on his left has the right-of-way.

Competitors may only repair or replace or exchange skis, sticks, straps or any other part of their equipment by means of a repairing outfit or spare parts which they are carrying with them during the race.

No competitor may borrow any portion of his equipment from a spectator.

A competitor who breaks or loses a ski may finish on a single ski, but a competitor who finishes without either ski will be disqualified.

A competitor will be disqualified if he puts his two sticks together, or if he holds a single stick, or both sticks in two hands, or if he seeks in any other way to evade the clear intention of this rule, i. e., to prevent competitors using their sticks as a means of reducing their speed. In other words, he cannot ride his ski poles.

Competitors are advised not to take unnecessary chances. The injury of a single competitor in this race will greatly detract from the sport of skiing.

THE RACE COMMITTEE.

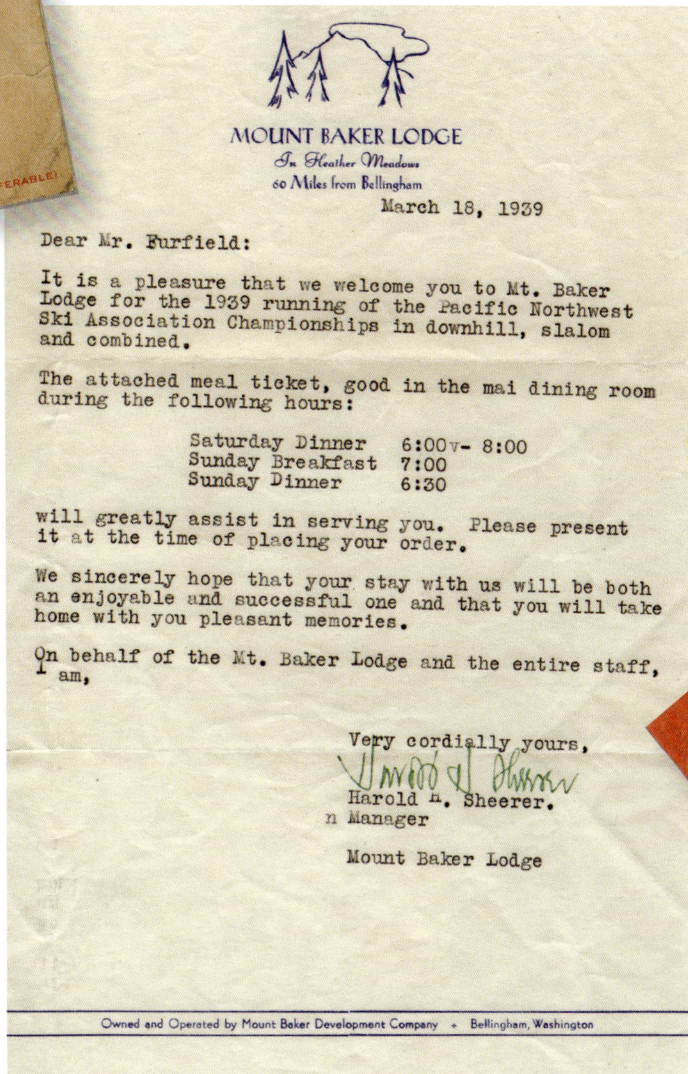

MOUNT BAKER LODGE
In Heather Meadows
60 Miles from Bellingham

March 18, 1939

Dear Mr. Furfield:

It is a pleasure that we welcome you to Mt. Baker Lodge for the 1939 running of the Pacific Northwest Ski Association Championships in downhill, slalom and combined.

The attached meal ticket, good in the mai dining room during the following hours:

Saturday Dinner	6:00v- 8:00
Sunday Breakfast	7:00
Sunday Dinner	6:30

will greatly assist in serving you. Please present it at the time of placing your order.

We sincerely hope that your stay with us will be both an enjoyable and successful one and that you will take home with you pleasant memories.

On behalf of the Mt. Baker Lodge and the entire staff, I am,

Very cordially yours,

Harold H. Sheerer.
n Manager

Mount Baker Lodge

Owned and Operated by Mount Baker Development Company • Bellingham, Washington

Most of Harry's ski competitions were in British Columbia but he did participate in events in the northwest United States, including Mount Baker, Snoqualmie Summit and Leavenworth, Washington.

Checking Skis – Snow Train Chuffs

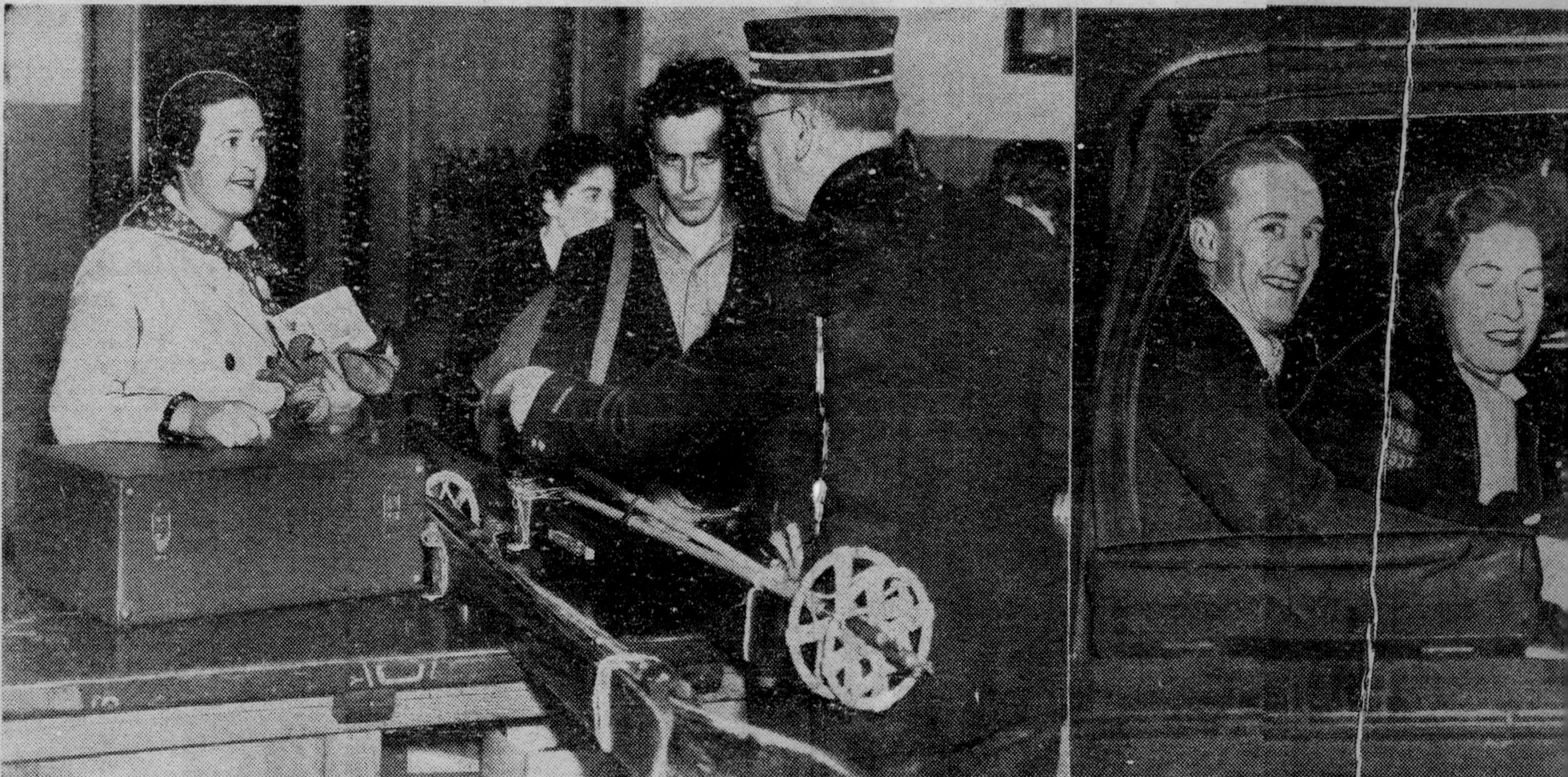

There was much excitement at the C.P.R. depot last evening as Vancouver's contingent of skiers climbed aboard the Snow Train which headed for Princeton and the Western Canadian Ski Championships. Many well-wishers including Mayor Miller were on hand to send the competitors and rooters on their merry way. Above on the left is a scene as the skiers check their highly important skis which have to be packed away very carefully to guard against injury are Dona McClay, Harry Burfiel centre picture is seen to what ex

Y 4, 1938

way – Fond Farewell

ip. Left to right the checkers
C.P.R. baggageman. In the
iers took over the train. Seen
in the cab of the locomotive are Art Hullah and Marg Lewis. There was also many a fond farewell. The cameraman sneaked up on this pair for a typical shot of the goings-on.—Photos by W. B. Shelly, Sun Staff Cameraman

Courtesy of The Vancouver Sun

In the 1930s and 1940s, Harry and his fellow competitors often traveled through the BC interior on ski trains that took them to the many racing and jumping events. The sport had become so popular that they had to settle for train cars as their accommodation because it was so difficult to find places to stay. Harry is shown in the picture on the left, looking at the camera while loading his skis and poles.

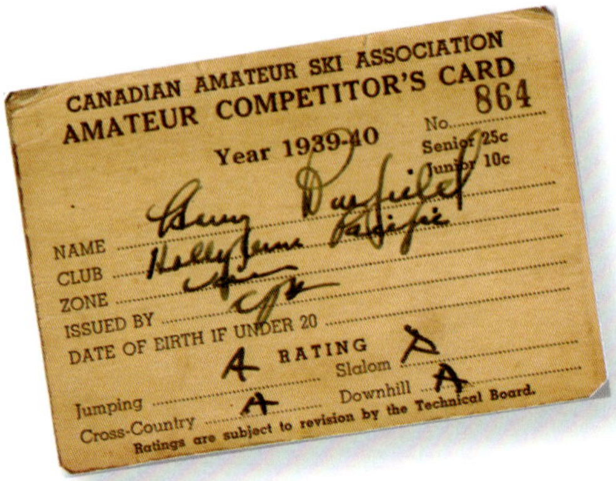

On Feb 9, 1940, in Leavenworth, WA, Harry, represented the Hollyburn Pacific Ski Club in a Class A division and placed 17th out of 22 competitors.

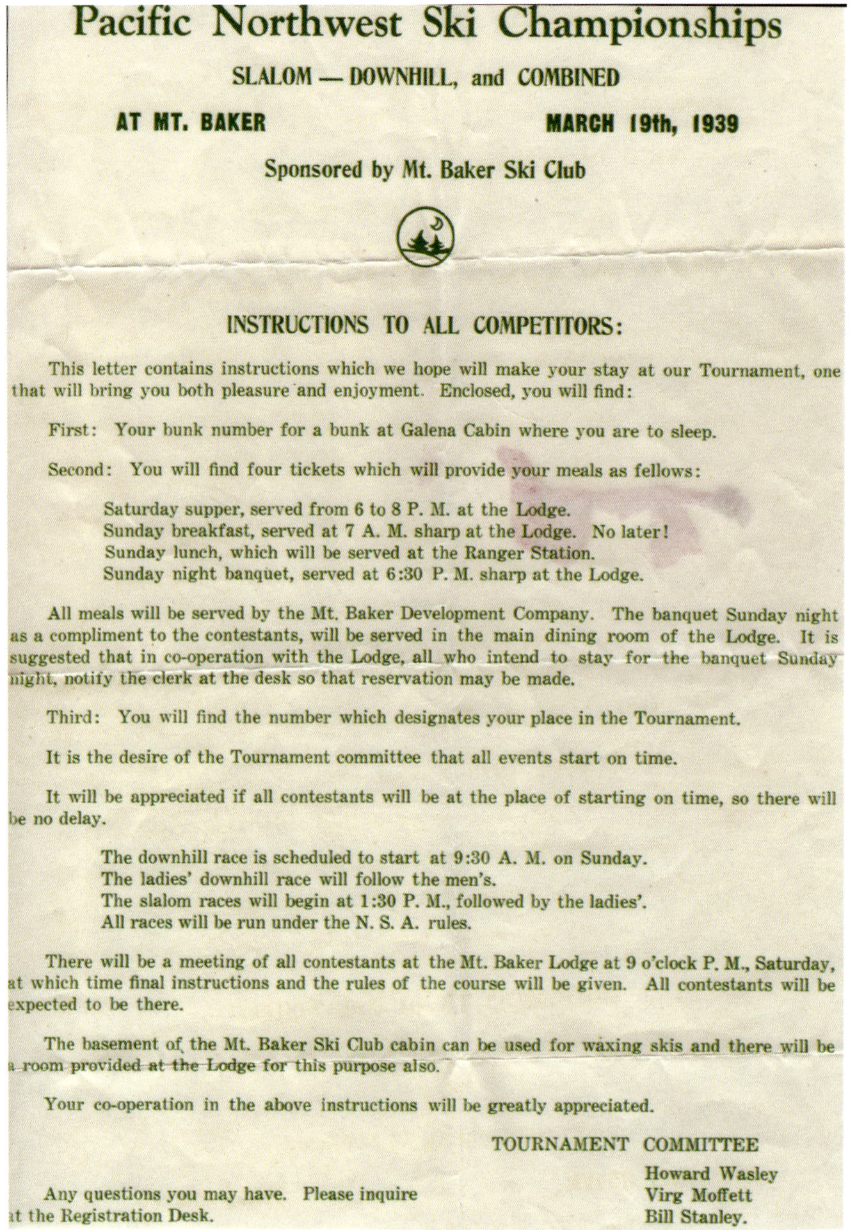

Pacific Northwest Ski Championships

SLALOM — DOWNHILL, and COMBINED

AT MT. BAKER **MARCH 19th, 1939**

Sponsored by Mt. Baker Ski Club

INSTRUCTIONS TO ALL COMPETITORS:

This letter contains instructions which we hope will make your stay at our Tournament, one that will bring you both pleasure and enjoyment. Enclosed, you will find:

First: Your bunk number for a bunk at Galena Cabin where you are to sleep.

Second: You will find four tickets which will provide your meals as fellows:

Saturday supper, served from 6 to 8 P. M. at the Lodge.
Sunday breakfast, served at 7 A. M. sharp at the Lodge. No later!
Sunday lunch, which will be served at the Ranger Station.
Sunday night banquet, served at 6:30 P. M. sharp at the Lodge.

All meals will be served by the Mt. Baker Development Company. The banquet Sunday night as a compliment to the contestants, will be served in the main dining room of the Lodge. It is suggested that in co-operation with the Lodge, all who intend to stay for the banquet Sunday night, notify the clerk at the desk so that reservation may be made.

Third: You will find the number which designates your place in the Tournament.

It is the desire of the Tournament committee that all events start on time.

It will be appreciated if all contestants will be at the place of starting on time, so there will be no delay.

The downhill race is scheduled to start at 9:30 A. M. on Sunday.
The ladies' downhill race will follow the men's.
The slalom races will begin at 1:30 P. M., followed by the ladies'.
All races will be run under the N. S. A. rules.

There will be a meeting of all contestants at the Mt. Baker Lodge at 9 o'clock P. M., Saturday, at which time final instructions and the rules of the course will be given. All contestants will be expected to be there.

The basement of the Mt. Baker Ski Club cabin can be used for waxing skis and there will be a room provided at the Lodge for this purpose also.

Your co-operation in the above instructions will be greatly appreciated.

TOURNAMENT COMMITTEE
Howard Wasley
Virg Moffett
Bill Stanley.

Any questions you may have. Please inquire at the Registration Desk.

RINCETON LAD SPEEDS TO REVELSTOKE VICTORY

SPORTS

HE VANCOUVER DAILY PROVINCE

ge Sixteen SATURDAY, FEBRUARY 11, 1939

Lew Davis Second to Bert Irwin In Western Championship Slalom

Fastest Times Made by "F. I. S. Amateurs," Peter Vadja and Norman Knight.

By DON TYRELL.
(Daily Province Staff Correspondent.)

REVELSTOKE.—Steel-edged skis flashing in the sun as they bit into the icy slalom hill, young Bert Irwin of the Amber Ski Club whizzed down the 2000-foot slope and won the Western Canadian amateur title Friday in two fast runs.

The twenty-year-old youth who has been his own coach and tutor, led one of the classiest fields ever to compete for the western title. His time of 2.42 was only a few seconds slower than Peter Vadja, Swiss coach of Vancouver's Tyee Ski Runners, who beat out Norman Knight, another "F.I.S. amateur" competing for the ski runners of the Canadian Rockies. These "F.I.S. amateurs" are not eligible for the championship.

Vadja found the icy slopes very much like those of his native Switzerland, and turned in the fastest time of the day, 1.09, for his second effort.

Lew Davis, pupil of Vadja's, was the first Vancouver boy in the money, finishing second to Irwin less than three seconds behind him.

Third place in the men's slalom went to another member of the Irwin family, eighteen-year-old Bill, who lacks only a little competitive experience to be one of the leading racers in the entire Northwest.

Fell Four Times

Gertie Wepsala, holder of most of Canada's women's ski titles, made good again Friday by winning the women's downhill. Despite the fact that she had four falls on the way down, the little Tyee star turned in a time of 1.49.6 to nose out Hollyburn Pacific's Daisy Bourdon by less than a second. The champion made a truly wonderful run, and a fall right at the finish when she failed to see the proper finishing spot, cost her about ten seconds.

Gertie Surprised By Sister Elmi

REVELSTOKE. — Elmi Teppo, Tyee ski runner of Vancouver, scored the first major upset of the Western Canadian ski championships when she won the women's slalom race here this morning, beating her sister Gertie Wepsala, national champion, who was the pre-race favorite. Elmi's time, 1 minute 2 seconds, was twenty seconds faster to turn in the fastest time of the day, 53 seconds. Daisy Bourdon, Hollyburn Pacific Ski Club of Vancouver, placed third.

She crashed into the crowd, scattering spectators on every side.

Peggy Mobraaten, Vancouver Ski Club, finished third in 1.55.2.

By the time the men had finished their slalom race the hill was iron-crusted. The scrape of skis on ice could be heard at the bottom. The angle of the hill, about forty degrees, was so steep that when a racer spilled she would slide a hundred yards at least before stopping.

Twenty-six "A" class jumpers went into action today. Revelstoke Ski Club, without a doubt the hardest working club this

Some of the many newspaper articles Harry saved about his skiing accomplishments as well as those of his competitors.

Courtesy of The Vancouver Daily Province

The women skiers had to compete at the same level as the men on some of the toughest runs.

Gertie Surprised By Sister Elmi

REVELSTOKE. — Elmi Teppo, Tyee ski runner of Vancouver, scored the first major upset of the Western Canadian ski championships when she won the women's slalom race here this morning, beating her sister Gertie Wepsala, national champion, who was the pre-race favorite. Elmi's time, 1 minute 2 seconds, was twenty seconds faster to turn in the fastest time of the day, 53 seconds. Daisy Bourdon, Hollyburn Pacific Ski Club of Vancouver, placed third.

She crashed into the crowd, scattering spectators on every side.

Peggy Mobraaten, Vancouver Ski Club, finished third in 1.55.2.

By the time the men had finished their slalom race the hill was iron-crusted. The scrape of skis on ice could be heard at the bottom. The angle of the hill, about forty degrees, was so steep that when a racer spilled she would slide a hundred yards at least before stopping.

Twenty-six "A" class jumpers went into action today. Revelstoke Ski Club, without a doubt the hardest working club this writer has ever seen, have the big jump in first class shape. We like Tom Mobraaten to win, he is the logical choice on his consistent past performances.

MEN'S SLALOM.

P. Vadja (F.I.S.)	2.36.4
N. Knight (F.I.S.)	2.37.6
B. Irwin (A.S.C.)	2.42.6
L. Davis (T.S.R.)	2.45
W. Irwin (A.S.C.)	2.47.2
J. Bird (F. I. S.)	2.47.8
H. Davidson	3.07.6
J. Lindsay (V.W.S.C.)	3.08.2
W. Round	3.13.6
H. Gunnarson (R.S.C.)	3.36
H. Burfield (H.P.S.C.)	3.38.6
H. Armstrong (C.S.C.)	3.42
T. Mobraaten(V.S.C.)	3.42.2
D. McCrae	3.42.4
A. Coles (T.S.R.)	3.46.8

WOMEN'S DOWNHILL.

G. Wepsala (T.S.R.)	1.49.6
D. Bourdon (H.S.P.C.)	1.50.8
P. Mobraaten (V.S.C.)	1.55.2
Ainsworth (V.S.C.)	2.06.4
[illegible] (C.M.S.C.)	[illegible]

SKI SCENE—Silhouetted against a bright sky, a competitor waits his turn at the top of the slalom course at Revelstoke. A mere 3000 feet below, down a nice grade, can be seen a small group at the finish line. On the left, Peter Vadja of the Tyee Ski Runners takes a fast turn through the stakes on his way to a new record for the course, a feat which brought him the "open" championship. Bottom left, our own Gertie Wepsala is seen as she flashed across the line, winning the women's downhill race. On the right, Norm Knight, who finished one second behind, Vadja does an ups-a-Daisy as he makes a quick turn at the finish. Behind him can be seen the full sweep of the tricky slalom course.

Army of Skiers Get Big Send-Off By Local Friends

Mayor Miller Starts Vancouver Contingent On Way to Princeton

By Canadian Press

Vancouver's picked skiing contingent neared Princeton today, ready to don their boards and take to the hills and the big jump in the Western Canada ski championships this week-end.

Behind them were the cheers and good wishes of friends who gathered at the railway depot last night to see them off. Ahead of them was three days' competition against the top-notch skiers of the Pacific Northwest.

Their departure was one of the most colorful in Vancouver sports history. The travelers were decked out in their newest sports toggery—jackets, parkas, spats and other finery which makes skiers among the best dressed of all athletes.

Vancouver's Mayor G. C. Miller, a recent skiing convert and newly-elected honorary president of the Grouse Mountain Tyee ski runners, was on hand to wish his club members goodbye, and express his hope they'd have "all the luck in the world."

The feature of the trip so far as most of the skiers is concerned, is that the "snow train" on which they left Vancouver last night, will be their home for three days at Princeton. The novel idea will save expenses and reduce overcrowding in Princeton hotels.

Reports from Princeton today said more than 100 skiers would take part n cross country, slalom, downhill and umping events. Most of the entrants ill be from the Pacific Coast, but terior towns — Revelstoke, Nelson, asland. Oliver, Wells, Vernon and ers—will also be represented.

LARGE CROWD GREETS VANCOUVER SNOW TRAIN TODAY

Below Zero Temperatures Completely Disregarded as Visitors Are Welcomed to Big Western Canada Ski Meet.

Notwithstanding the fact that thermometers in the vicinity registered 1[illegible] degrees below zero, the Canadian Pacific Railway platform was thronged from beginning to end with local residents, visiting tournament spectators, and competitors, when the special ski train arrived from Vancouver this morning.

The train left Vancouver last night jollied by a big good-natured crowd of well-wishers. The departure was broadcast by Vancouver radio station CKWX. The portable pack transmitters were among the equipment with which events of the tournament will be broadcast. Bob Tweedie, noted Vancouver skier, will do the commentating.

Motion picture cameras clicked and amateur photographers jostled each other to get points of vantage from which to record the arrival.

Half a dozen sleighs, pulled by horse with plenty of "jingle bells," took the visitors down town, from where they dispersed to various eating places.

One arrival, masquerading as a large snow man, walked up and down the platform, to add a touch of comedy to the scene, already hilarious and jolly with the shouting multitude.

Mayor Walter Hardman, Frank Allwood, president of the Board of Trade, mixed with the crowd, welcoming as many of the visitors, individually, as possible.

The three tourist sleepers will be parked here as auxiliary hotel accommodation until they return with the contingent, Sunday night.

'B' CLASS SKIER UPSETS EXPERTS

Taking personal control of a race that had been planned as a workout for the Hollyburn Pacific Ski Club's Banff team, Harry Burfield came whisking down the Ridge downhill course Sunday afternoon to capture first place from the finest downhill runners in the club.

Just promoted from the ranks of the B Class racers, Burfield defeated the picked plankmen who will represent the club in the Dominion championships, tearing down from the peak in a minute and 59 seconds. Behind him Irish Beaumont, rated the best of the Hollyburn skiers, Ace Lindsay, Banff team member, and Bill Brown, finished second, third and fourth. Beaumont made the run in 2.02 and Lindsay was clocked in 2.14.

In the B Class race, from the Shoulder, Norm Fiddler was first in 1.23; Jack Pratt second in 1.32 and Stan Harrison third in 1.36. Margaret Gale won the women's event in 1.46 with Tess Murby second and Jean McCurdy third.

Saturday night more than 200 attended a dance held in the club cabin to raise funds to be used in assisting the club team in the trip to Banff.

Harrys 1st First Aid Certifiicate. He felt it was neccessary in case of any accidents on the ski hills.

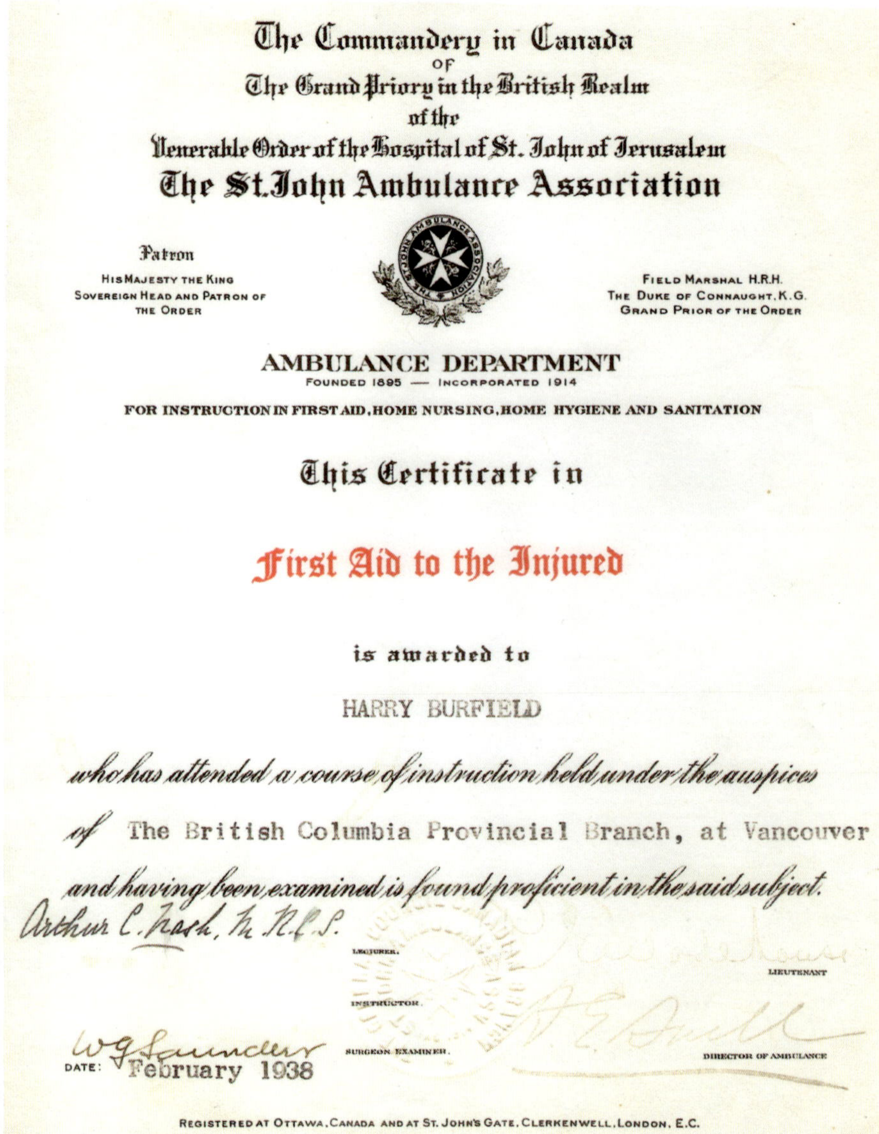

The Commandery in Canada
OF
The Grand Priory in the British Realm
of the
Venerable Order of the Hospital of St. John of Jerusalem
The St. John Ambulance Association

Patron
His Majesty the King
Sovereign Head and Patron of the Order

Field Marshal H.R.H.
The Duke of Connaught, K.G.
Grand Prior of the Order

AMBULANCE DEPARTMENT
Founded 1895 — Incorporated 1914

FOR INSTRUCTION IN FIRST AID, HOME NURSING, HOME HYGIENE AND SANITATION

This Certificate in

First Aid to the Injured

is awarded to

HARRY BURFIELD

who has attended a course of instruction held under the auspices of The British Columbia Provincial Branch, at Vancouver and having been examined is found proficient in the said subject.

Arthur C. Nash, M.R.C.S.
LECTURER.
INSTRUCTOR.
W G Saunders
SURGEON EXAMINER.
LIEUTENANT
DIRECTOR OF AMBULANCE
DATE: February 1938

Registered at Ottawa, Canada and at St. John's Gate, Clerkenwell, London, E.C.

Seattle Ski Club

NINTH
Annual Tournament
(Open Tournament)

SNOQUALMIE SUMMIT
Sunday, March 6, 1938

Roy Nerland
Tournament Manager
Howard Dalsbo
Hill Captain

JUDGES

Reidar Gjolme
Seattle, Wn.

Harald Lee
Portland, Ore.

Rolf Syversen
Vancouver, B. C.

PHYSICIANS

Dr. Ivar Birkeland

Dr. D. Metheny

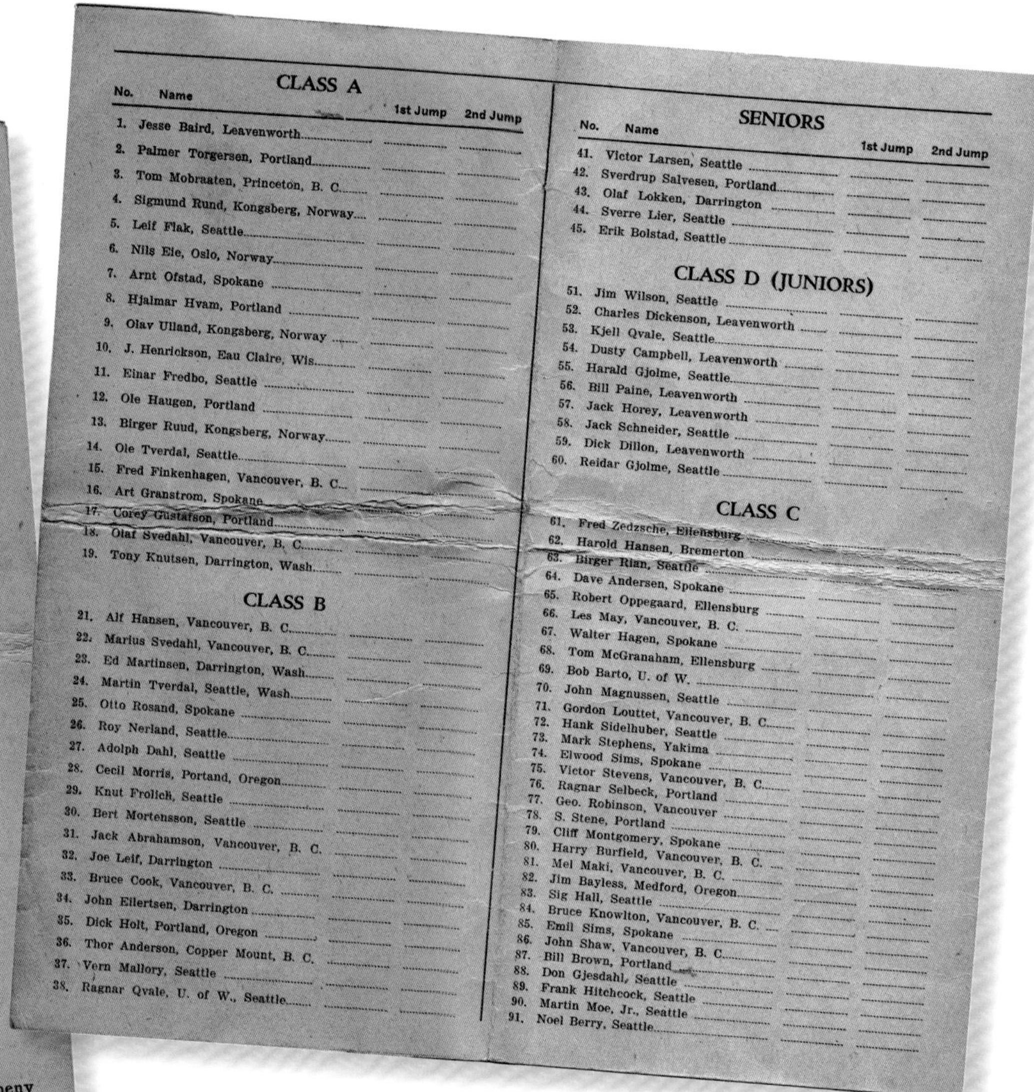

CLASS A

No.	Name	1st Jump	2nd Jump
1.	Jesse Baird, Leavenworth		
2.	Palmer Torgersen, Portland		
3.	Tom Mobraaten, Princeton, B. C.		
4.	Sigmund Rund, Kongsberg, Norway		
5.	Leif Flak, Seattle		
6.	Nils Eie, Oslo, Norway		
7.	Arnt Ofstad, Spokane		
8.	Hjalmar Hvam, Portland		
9.	Olav Ulland, Kongsberg, Norway		
10.	J. Henrickson, Eau Claire, Wis.		
11.	Einar Fredbo, Seattle		
12.	Ole Haugen, Portland		
13.	Birger Ruud, Kongsberg, Norway		
14.	Ole Tverdal, Seattle		
15.	Fred Finkenhagen, Vancouver, B. C.		
16.	Art Granstrom, Spokane		
17.	Corey Gustafson, Portland		
18.	Olaf Svedahl, Vancouver, B. C.		
19.	Tony Knutsen, Darrington, Wash.		

CLASS B

No.	Name	1st Jump	2nd Jump
21.	Alf Hansen, Vancouver, B. C.		
22.	Marius Svedahl, Vancouver, B. C.		
23.	Ed Martinsen, Darrington, Wash.		
24.	Martin Tverdal, Seattle, Wash.		
25.	Otto Rosand, Spokane		
26.	Roy Nerland, Seattle		
27.	Adolph Dahl, Seattle		
28.	Cecil Morris, Portand, Oregon		
29.	Knut Frolich, Seattle		
30.	Bert Mortensson, Seattle		
31.	Jack Abrahamson, Vancouver, B. C.		
32.	Joe Leif, Darrington		
33.	Bruce Cook, Vancouver, B. C.		
34.	John Ellertsen, Darrington		
35.	Dick Holt, Portland, Oregon		
36.	Thor Anderson, Copper Mount, B. C.		
37.	Vern Mallory, Seattle		
38.	Ragnar Qvale, U. of W., Seattle		

SENIORS

No.	Name	1st Jump	2nd Jump
41.	Victor Larsen, Seattle		
42.	Sverdrup Salvesen, Portland		
43.	Olaf Lokken, Darrington		
44.	Sverre Lier, Seattle		
45.	Erik Bolstad, Seattle		

CLASS D (JUNIORS)

No.	Name	1st Jump	2nd Jump
51.	Jim Wilson, Seattle		
52.	Charles Dickenson, Leavenworth		
53.	Kjell Qvale, Seattle		
54.	Dusty Campbell, Leavenworth		
55.	Harald Gjolme, Seattle		
56.	Bill Paine, Leavenworth		
57.	Jack Horey, Leavenworth		
58.	Jack Schneider, Seattle		
59.	Dick Dillon, Leavenworth		
60.	Reidar Gjolme, Seattle		

CLASS C

No.	Name	1st Jump	2nd Jump
61.	Fred Zedzsche, Ellensburg		
62.	Harold Hansen, Bremerton		
63.	Birger Rian, Seattle		
64.	Dave Andersen, Spokane		
65.	Robert Oppegaard, Ellensburg		
66.	Les May, Vancouver, B. C.		
67.	Walter Hagen, Spokane		
68.	Tom McGranaham, Ellensburg		
69.	Bob Barto, U. of W.		
70.	John Magnussen, Seattle		
71.	Gordon Louttet, Vancouver, B. C.		
72.	Hank Sidelhuber, Seattle		
73.	Mark Stephens, Yakima		
74.	Elwood Sims, Spokane		
75.	Victor Stevens, Vancouver, B. C.		
76.	Ragnar Selbeck, Portland		
77.	Geo. Robinson, Vancouver		
78.	S. Stene, Portland		
79.	Cliff Montgomery, Spokane		
80.	Harry Burfield, Vancouver, B. C.		
81.	Mel Maki, Vancouver, B. C.		
82.	Jim Bayless, Medford, Oregon		
83.	Sig Hall, Seattle		
84.	Bruce Knowlton, Vancouver, B. C.		
85.	Emil Sims, Spokane		
86.	John Shaw, Vancouver, B. C.		
87.	Bill Brown, Portland		
88.	Don Gjesdahl, Seattle		
89.	Frank Hitchcock, Seattle		
90.	Martin Moe, Jr., Seattle		
91.	Noel Berry, Seattle		

Third
annual open
ROSE
FESTIVAL
SKI
TOURNAMENT
TIMBERLINE LODGE
MT. HOOD, OREGON
JUNE 12, 1938
Sponsored by
OREGON WINTER
SPORTS ASS'N.
Under the auspices of
CASCADE SKI
CLUB
"for you a rose
in Portland grows"
TIMBERLINE LODGE
Mt. Hood, Oregon
You'll hear
a lot of argument
and difference of opinion about the proper length of skis and the
way to do a "christie". But, there's one skiing item on which
we're all agreed and that's
PENDLETON
Shirts
You can take a Pendleton-climb clear to the top. If the day's hot, you're
protected from the sun; if it's cold, those same pure virgin wool fibres go
into reverse and keep you fireside-warm. You don't lose any action in a
Pendleton, either, because they're cut roomy—styled right—and built to
give a lifetime of lasting satisfaction.
Golfers wear them for their comfort and good looks—fishermen and
hunters for their warmth and action freedom—sportsmen everywhere
choose Pendletons for all outdoor activity. If you don't own a Pendleton,
go to your favorite sports or department store, ask to see one—you'll agree
with the thousands there's nothing like
PENDLETON
Shirts
At leading stores . . . five to ten dollars
PENDLETON WOOLEN MILLS
PORTLAND, OREGON
Organizing Committee
HARRY SWART
President, Oregon Winter Sports Association
FRED McNEIL
President, Cascade Ski Club
A. O. WAHA
Supervisor, Mt. Hood National Forest
HORACE MECKLEM
Vice-President, Timberline Lodge, Inc.
Committee in Charge
BOYD FRENCH
General Chairman
GEORGE HENDERSON
Promotion Director
FRED VAN DYKE
Chief Timer
JACK GREENWOOD
Decorations and Traffic
ROY K. TERRY
Junior Skiers
BUD NOCK
Co-Chairman
HARRY STEVENS
Entries
JIM MOUNT
Accommodations
Race Committee
BOYD FRENCH
Chief of Course
HAROLD ENGLES
Chief Starter
JIM SIMMONS
Assistant Starter
ROY K. TERRY
Assistant Starter
DR. PAUL SPANGLER
First Aid
WARD IRWIN
Registration
FRED VAN DYKE
Chief Timer
LYNN DARCY
Assistant Timer
HAROLD HANSON
Assistant Timer
HAL KELLEY
Chief Recorder
MRS. FRED VAN DYKE
Assistant Recorder
MARGIE FRENCH SIMMONS
Assistant Recorder
NOTE: It is necessary that spectators protect their eyes and complexions from sunburn or snow-burn.
The Oregon Winter Sports Association and Cascade Ski Club wish to express their appreciation
to the following for their courtesy and assistance in the conduct of this tournament.
Mr. Berger Underdahl
Mr. E. J. Griffith, W.P.A. Administrator
Mr. C. J. Buck, Regional Forester
Mr. H. V. Horton, Assistant Regional Forester
Major James A. Franklin, Asst. Regional Forester
Portland Junior Chamber of Commerce
The committee is especially indebted to the Standard Oil Company of California
for their cooperation in furnishing the public address system for today's program
Instructions for Competitors
Competitors shall report for registration and receive numbers not later than 10:00 a. m. Sunday morning in the Ski Lounge of Timberline Lodge.
The courses will be set Saturday, June 11, by Chief of Course, Boyd French.
The FIS (Federation Internationale De Ski) Rules of Downhill Racing govern all of the races.
All races will employ the interval start, the racers being started at one minute intervals.
There are several control gates on the downhill course. The exact position and number of these control gates will be explained as they go up Sunday morning.
All control gates will be marked by BLUE and WHITE flags and competitors must pass between the control flags or be disqualified.
An advisory course is marked out by flags. Other than passing between the indicated control gates it is not necessary to follow the flagged course.
A competitor in a One Way Section (such as the track made by the snow plough) who shall be on the point of being overtaken shall step out of the track on hearing the warning cry of the overtaking competitor. A competitor who under these circumstances shall refuse to step out of the track shall be disqualified.
The course will be closed for practice on Sunday morning. Any competitor running the course thereafter shall be disqualified.
Competitors may only repair or replace or exchange skis, sticks, straps or any other part of their equipment by means of a repairing outfit or spare parts which they are carrying with them during the race.
No competitor may borrow any portion of his equipment from a spectator.
A competitor who breaks or loses a ski may finish on a single ski, but a competitor who finishes without either ski will be disqualified.
A competitor shall be disqualified if he puts his two sticks together, or if he holds a single stick, or both sticks in two hands, or if he seeks in any other way to evade the clear intention of this rule, i.e., to prevent competitors using their sticks, as a means of reducing their speed. In other words, he cannot ride his ski poles.
Competitors are advised not to take unnecessary chances. The injury of a single competitor in this race will greatly detract from the sport of skiing.
THE RACE COMMITTEE.

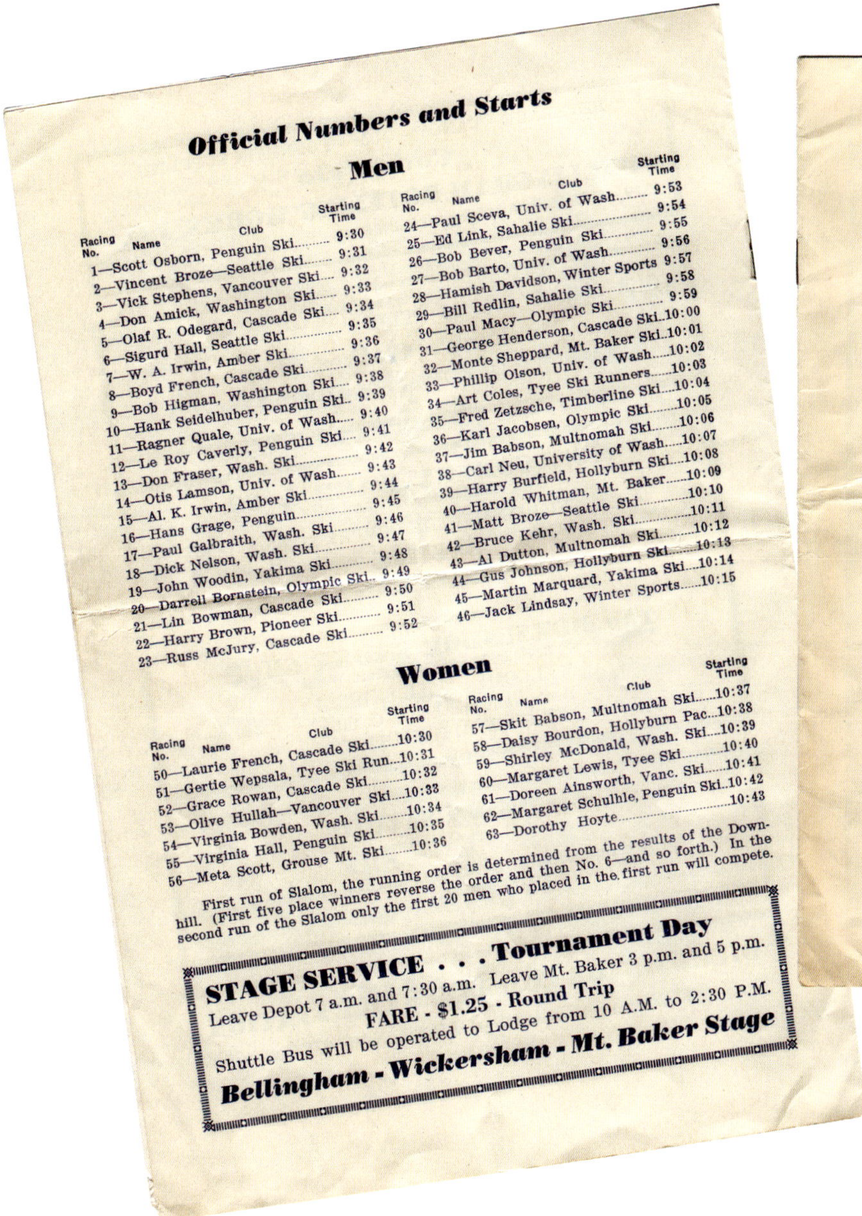

Official Numbers and Starts

Men

Racing No.	Name — Club	Starting Time
1	Scott Osborn, Penguin Ski	9:30
2	Vincent Broze—Seattle Ski	9:31
3	Vick Stephens, Vancouver Ski	9:32
4	Don Amick, Washington Ski	9:33
5	Olaf R. Odegard, Cascade Ski	9:34
6	Sigurd Hall, Seattle Ski	9:35
7	W. A. Irwin, Amber Ski	9:36
8	Boyd French, Cascade Ski	9:37
9	Bob Higman, Washington Ski	9:38
10	Hank Seidelhuber, Penguin Ski	9:39
11	Ragner Quale, Univ. of Wash.	9:40
12	Le Roy Caverly, Penguin Ski	9:41
13	Don Fraser, Wash. Ski	9:42
14	Otis Lamson, Univ. of Wash.	9:43
15	Al. K. Irwin, Amber Ski	9:44
16	Hans Grage, Penguin	9:45
17	Paul Galbraith, Wash. Ski	9:46
18	Dick Nelson, Wash. Ski	9:47
19	John Woodin, Yakima Ski	9:48
20	Darrell Bornstein, Olympic Ski	9:49
21	Lin Bowman, Cascade Ski	9:50
22	Harry Brown, Pioneer Ski	9:51
23	Russ McJury, Cascade Ski	9:52
24	Paul Sceva, Univ. of Wash.	9:53
25	Ed Link, Sahalie Ski	9:54
26	Bob Bever, Penguin Ski	9:55
27	Bob Barto, Univ. of Wash.	9:56
28	Hamish Davidson, Winter Sports	9:57
29	Bill Redlin, Sahalie Ski	9:58
30	Paul Macy—Olympic Ski	9:59
31	George Henderson, Cascade Ski	10:00
32	Monte Sheppard, Mt. Baker Ski	10:01
33	Phillip Olson, Univ. of Wash.	10:02
34	Art Coles, Tyee Ski Runners	10:03
35	Fred Zetzsche, Timberline Ski	10:04
36	Karl Jacobsen, Olympic Ski	10:05
37	Jim Babson, Multnomah Ski	10:06
38	Carl Neu, University of Wash.	10:07
39	Harry Burfield, Hollyburn Ski	10:08
40	Harold Whitman, Mt. Baker	10:09
41	Matt Broze—Seattle Ski	10:10
42	Bruce Kehr, Wash. Ski	10:11
43	Al Dutton, Multnomah Ski	10:12
44	Gus Johnson, Hollyburn Ski	10:13
45	Martin Marquard, Yakima Ski	10:14
46	Jack Lindsay, Winter Sports	10:15

Women

Racing No.	Name — Club	Starting Time
50	Laurie French, Cascade Ski	10:30
51	Gertie Wepsala, Tyee Ski Run	10:31
52	Grace Rowan, Cascade Ski	10:32
53	Olive Hullah—Vancouver Ski	10:33
54	Virginia Bowden, Wash. Ski	10:34
55	Virginia Hall, Penguin Ski	10:35
56	Meta Scott, Grouse Mt. Ski	10:36
57	Skit Babson, Multnomah Ski	10:37
58	Daisy Bourdon, Hollyburn Pac.	10:38
59	Shirley McDonald, Wash. Ski	10:39
60	Margaret Lewis, Tyee Ski	10:40
61	Doreen Ainsworth, Vanc. Ski	10:41
62	Margaret Schulhle, Penguin Ski	10:42
63	Dorothy Hoyte	10:43

First run of Slalom, the running order is determined from the results of the Downhill. (First five place winners reverse the order and then No. 6—and so forth.) In the second run of the Slalom only the first 20 men who placed in the first run will compete.

STAGE SERVICE . . . Tournament Day

Leave Depot 7 a.m. and 7:30 a.m. Leave Mt. Baker 3 p.m. and 5 p.m.

FARE - $1.25 - Round Trip

Shuttle Bus will be operated to Lodge from 10 A.M. to 2:30 P.M.

Bellingham - Wickersham - Mt. Baker Stage

P. N. S. A. CHAMPIONSHIPS

IN DOWNHILL AND SLALOM AND COMBINED

March 19, 1939

AUSPICES OF MT. BAKER SKI CLUB and MT. BAKER DEVELOPMENT COMPANY

UNION PRINTING CO., BELLINGHAM, WASH.

Mobraaten Hits Form; Johnny Leeds Injured

New Hill Proves Hard on Ski Equipment; Downhill Course Offers Tough Test.

By DON TYRELL.
(Daily Province Staff Correspondent.)

REVELSTOKE.—This railroad centre is all set to make its comeback as a "tournament town" this week. With the Western Canada ski championships scheduled to start Thursday morning, the whole town is behind the Revelstoke Ski Club and the Board of Trade determined to put the tourney over.

REVELSTOKE.—A word of advice to Vancouver skiers. This Revelstoke meet lines up as the best we've seen yet, so hock your extra pair of skis and leave with the gang Thursday night.

'Gertie Wepsala and your correspondent had their first ride in full command of a cutter sleigh this morning. We cantered through town behind one of Craig Rutherford's horses, feeling like something out of an 1890 family album.

Neither Gertie nor yours truly had the faintest idea of how to turn corners, let alone stop or start the darned thing. Tomorrow we take another try at it.

WATCH BERT IRWIN!

Competitive skiers are warned to watch Bert Irwin of the Amber Ski Club. While he was good last year, he is a vastly-improved skier now and has the necessary strength. Jack Pratt, youthful Hollyburner, has been doing nothing but ski with the Irwins at Princeton for the last month and his ski-ing has improved considerably. He is just waiting to get a crack at his old friend and tutor, Gus Johnson.

Gus Johnson.

Daisy Bourdon and Doreen Ainsworth were also going great guns. Doreen's ski-ing is just about 200 per cent. above her best efforts of previous years. We figure she has come faster this year than any other girl in the Vancouver Ski Club. She is really learning to control her "planks" now.

Milk seems to be the popular drink with the skiers at this meet. That may sound strange, but it's true. On the way up to the slalom and downhill runs this morning, a milkman, whose sled followed ours, sold practically all his stock to the thirsty skiers.

Nip Stone will have to publicly apologize for his advice about Revelstoke temperatures unless it gets considerably colder around here. Two more days of this sunshine and we'll be able to get a job as a cigar-store Indian.

Skiers are arriving on every train, although the first event is still a few days away. Visiting competitors are being given the treat of their lives by Revelstoke citizens. Ski-joring, behind cars and horses, is one of the most popular pastimes with Vancouver skiers. Riding behind smart little cutters, pulled by fast-moving horses, is giving even the more blase unexpected thrills.

The streets are covered with about three feet of dry snow; the tinkle of sleigh bells, and the fact that most of the citizens travel by sleigh or ski makes this one of the most colorful spots in the West.

Bright, warm sunshine, an oddity to Vancouver plankmen, is giving the early arrivals a healthy coat of tan. Ski-ing in shirt sleeves was popular Monday on the slalom and downhill courses.

TOM IS DOING WELL.

Visiting jumpers are having plenty of grief with the new Revelstoke hill. Three pairs of skis were broken Sunday and two on Monday. John Leeds, Copper Mountain star, injured his knee, and Vic Stevens, Vancouver Ski Club four-way man, suffered a badly-sprained ankle. The injuries to the Copper Mountain lad's knee may keep him out of the competition and cost him a trip to the ski-jumping event at the World's Fair in San Francisco.

Tom Mobraaten, white hope of the Viskies in the four-way point gathering, made two nice jumps in the neighborhood of 175 feet Monday. Hans Gunnarson of the Revelstoke Gunnarsons was reported to be getting even more distance in the afternoon.

IT'S REALLY FAST.

Favorite topic amongst the

Favorite topic amongst the skiers in town seemed to be the men's downhill course. En route to this city we had heard that the run averaged a grade of some thirty to thirty-eight degrees. As an average this seemed far too steep, but after looking at the course we can fully believe it more than lives up to its advance reputation.

With Kon Lien we skied over from the slalom course to look at the lower slope of the downhill route, supposed to be the easiest portion.

Korey Hegseth, an "A" class jumper, who has performed on many a big jumping hill, said he picked up more speed on this section than he had ever handled before.

The women's downhill race will be held over the same slope as the men's slalom. Officials figured the original plan to run them over part of the men's trail to be too dangerous. As the men's run has a drop of some 2200 feet in a mile and a quarter, this new policy seems to be wisest.

With steep wood-running over a bumpy ridge and a lightning schusse at the finish, the trail from high up the side of Mount Revelstoke will try the skill of the best runner in the tournament. The winner will need legs of steel to complete it in any sort of shape.

NELSON.—Hon. W. J. Asselstine, British Columbia minister of mines, has donated a new ski trophy for miners. The Asselstine Cup, to be competed for at the Western Canada ski meet in Revelstoke this week, is open to amateur skiers who are also miners in British Columbia.

The Irwin brothers jumping at Amber Ski Hill, Princeton, BC, one of the few places competitors jumped side-by-side.

20
FH911

Chapter Three

In Flight

Harry continued competing until he joined the Royal Canadian Air Force in 1943. During the Second World War, Harry trained as a pilot and was worked his way up to the rank of Sergeant. He kept in shape while he was in the Air Force by playing football and other sports. When the war ended in 1945, he took up where he left off and once again became an avid ski competitor.

facing page: Harry ready to take off in a Royal Canadian Air Force (RCAF) plane during his training to be a pilot.

Representing the Hollyburn Pacific Ski Club, Harry watches other competitors as he waits his turn, Princeton, 1940.

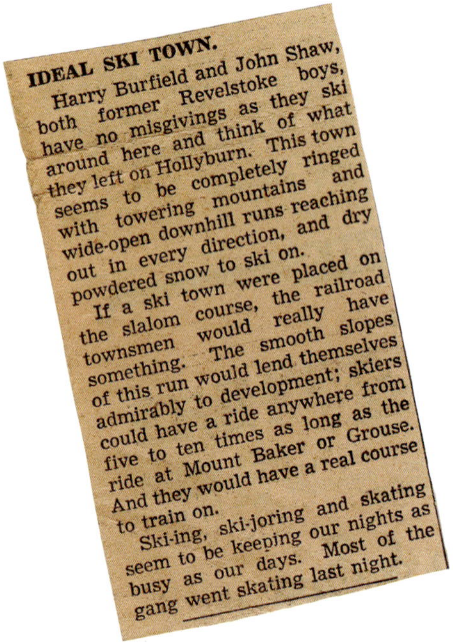

IDEAL SKI TOWN.

Harry Burfield and John Shaw, both former Revelstoke boys, have no misgivings as they ski around here and think of what they left on Hollyburn. This town seems to be completely ringed with towering mountains and wide-open downhill runs reaching out in every direction, and dry powdered snow to ski on.

If a ski town were placed on the slalom course, the railroad townsmen would really have something. The smooth slopes of this run would lend themselves admirably to development; skiers could have a ride anywhere from five to ten times as long as the ride at Mount Baker or Grouse. And they would have a real course to train on.

Ski-ing, ski-joring and skating seem to be keeping our nights as busy as our days. Most of the gang went skating last night.

Harry slalom racing. Skiers had to learn quickly in the past because of their rustic equipment. The poles they used were small trees that didn't bend. Not like the plastic, flexible ones they use today.

These photos were taken at the Hedley Mine (Canty Mine), near Hedley, BC, on highway number 3 between Princeton and Keremeos. The terrain at the mine is steep and scary! Harry has written a description on the back of each photograph.

Harry working at the Hedley Mine.

"Harry and I both worked at the mine in the 40s. Harry worked as a carpenter and I worked as a baker. When I first went there I wanted to work under ground but my baking became so popular that I was doubling up on my pies and cookies. One day there came in a new cook and he had forgotten my pies in the oven and burned them. It created a big fight in the kitchen and I finally got to go underground where I wanted to be!"

—Fred Burfield

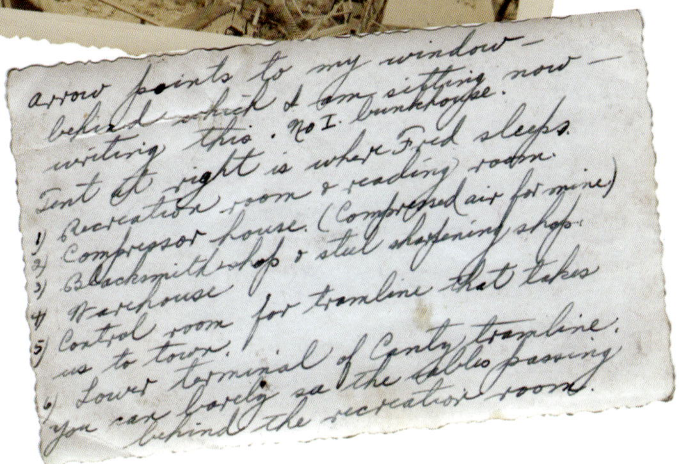
arrow points to my window—
behind which I am sitting now—
writing this. No I. bunkhouse.
Tent at right is where Fred sleeps.
1) Recreation room & reading room
2) Compressor house. (Compressed air for mine)
3) Blacksmith shop & steel sharpening shop.
4) Warehouse
5) Control room for tramline that takes
us to town.
6) Lower terminal of Canty tramline.
You can barely see the cables passing
behind the recreation room.

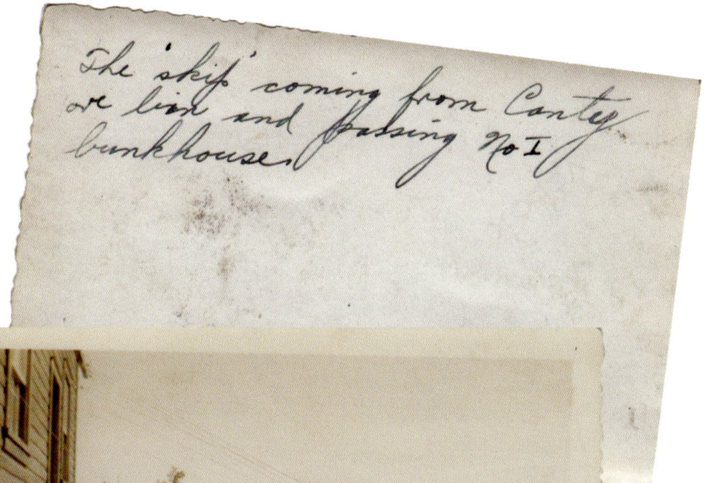
The 'skip' coming from Canty
ore bin and passing No I
bunkhouse.

The Commandery in Canada
of
The Grand Priory in the British Realm
of the
Venerable Order of the Hospital of St. John of Jerusalem
The St. John Ambulance Association

Patron
His Majesty the King
Sovereign Head and Patron of the Order

AMBULANCE DEPARTMENT

FOR INSTRUCTION IN FIRST AID, HOME NURSING, HOME HYGIENE AND SANITATION

This is to Certify that

HARRY BURFIELD

a certified pupil was Re-examined for the first time on

First Aid to the Injured

in the month of April 19, 1940 under the jurisdiction of

The British Columbia Provincial Branch, at Hedley

and has satisfied the Medical Examiner.

Issued by authority of the Lieutenant and the Director of Ambulance.

REGISTERED AT OTTAWA, CANADA AND AT ST. JOHN'S GATE, CLERKENWELL, LONDON, E.C.

The 2nd First Aid Certificate that Harry received. This one was for Headley Mines.

Harry up in the air where he felt the greatest. He loved what he did.

KING WINTER'S CHRISTMAS CARD—Like a scene from another world is this beautiful photograph of Heather Lodge in Mt. Revelstoke National Park. It seems to embody the very spirit of peace for which the world outside is striving. No artificial setting or stage could catch the beauty of a wild grandeur softened by the s this natural photograph gives. The pho Royal Canadian Air Force.

The original Heather Lodge, located on Revelstoke Mountain. This picture would have been taken in the 40s. It was a popular place for Harry to relax with friends. Later he vacationed there with his family. Marion Burfield remembers visiting the lodge and all the caves in the surrounding area when she was young. The kids were watched very closely by their parents as they liked to go exploring into the caves where the bears were hibernating for the winter months. They didn't want to wake them. Prince, the family dog, was once mistaken for a bear by visitors. One day he opened the door to the lodge with his nose and went strolling in. Several ladies who were playing cards at the table went screaming out the back door.

The Lodge was deliberately burned down in the 1960s because people were using it as a party hang-out and it was in very poor condition as a result. For everyones safety, the building had to come down.

Hollyburners this weekend are planning on a trip to Mt. Strachan the first of the season if the snow is in good condition. George Woods of Mt. Seymour says he would like to see what this back country looks like. Wonder how he missed this stretch, as he's been on every peak from Seymour to Garibaldi and back several times.

Harry Burfield, who topped the city skiers last week, is easy-going, so much so that driving his car with the gearshift waving around loose makes no difference, until it finally came right out and he merely laughed.

Hollyburn Skiers, Two Kimberleyites Visiting at Nelson

Harry Burfield of the Hollyburn Pacific Ski Club, Vancouver, a former Nelson and Revelstoke boy, spent Monday at Nelson renewing old acquaintances. He was the guest of Danny and Dee McKay, leading Nelson skiers. Burfield plans to leave this morning for Vancouver, where he will enter the Viskie classic race on Hollyburn. Later he will compete at the Western Canada meet at Wells.

Two Kimberley skiers, Pete Gallpen and Terry Gower, en route home from the Kootenay Zone Championships at Rossland, are also spending a couple of days here to try out the Nelson courses. Others of the large contingent of Kimberley skiers at the meet arrived in Nelson after banquet at Trail and left on the 1:30 a.m. train Monday for their home.

Burfield Second

Irwin Snaps Viski Classic Record

Young Billy Irwin added another trophy to his already filled cabinet when he swept over a tough Hollyburn Mt. course to cop top honors in the annual Viski classic yesterday.

Young Bill Irwin's name was on all skiers' lips yesterday after he had won the Viski classic race in record breaking time. Over an icy course Irwin didn't go down once and crossed the finish line safely ahead of second place Harry Burfield. Irwin is now in the Army.

The Princeton planker, now in the Irish Fusiliers, was in rare form and was about the only skier able to keep his feet while touring the two and one half miles.

Top man among the local plankers was Harry Burfield who, although he took a bad fall on the Romstead Hill, swept in for second place. His time broke the previous city record by 18 seconds.

Jack Pratt placed third and also snapped the record by a safe margin, but it still remained for Irwin's record breaking time and daring skiing to take the crowd's breath away.

Irwin snapped the former mark by 33 seconds.

There were 36 entrants in the Viski classic and the course was opened by two juniors, Paddy Wing and Jerry Lockhart.

The women's race will be run next week, but if yesterday's ski conditions prevail the races will be called off temporarily.

Bill Irwin	6.13.4
Harry Burfield, HPSC	6.28.4
Jack Pratt, HPSC	6.49.4
Ernie Griffith, Tyee	7.08.8
George Robinson, HPSC	7.11.8
Art Johnson, VSC	7.12.2
Ole Johanson, VSC	7.15
Henry Sotvedt, VSC	7.15.8
Karl Baadsvick, Tyee	7.29.8
Ed. Oakley, HPSC	7.49
Stan Body, GMSC	7.52.4
Bob Crosby, UBCSC	7.56

Parker in Form; Defeats Rea

Cliff Parker was in rare roughing form Sa[illegible]day night at the

Rossland, February 21st and 22nd, 1942 was a busy two days of competitions with many different classes of racing and jumping.

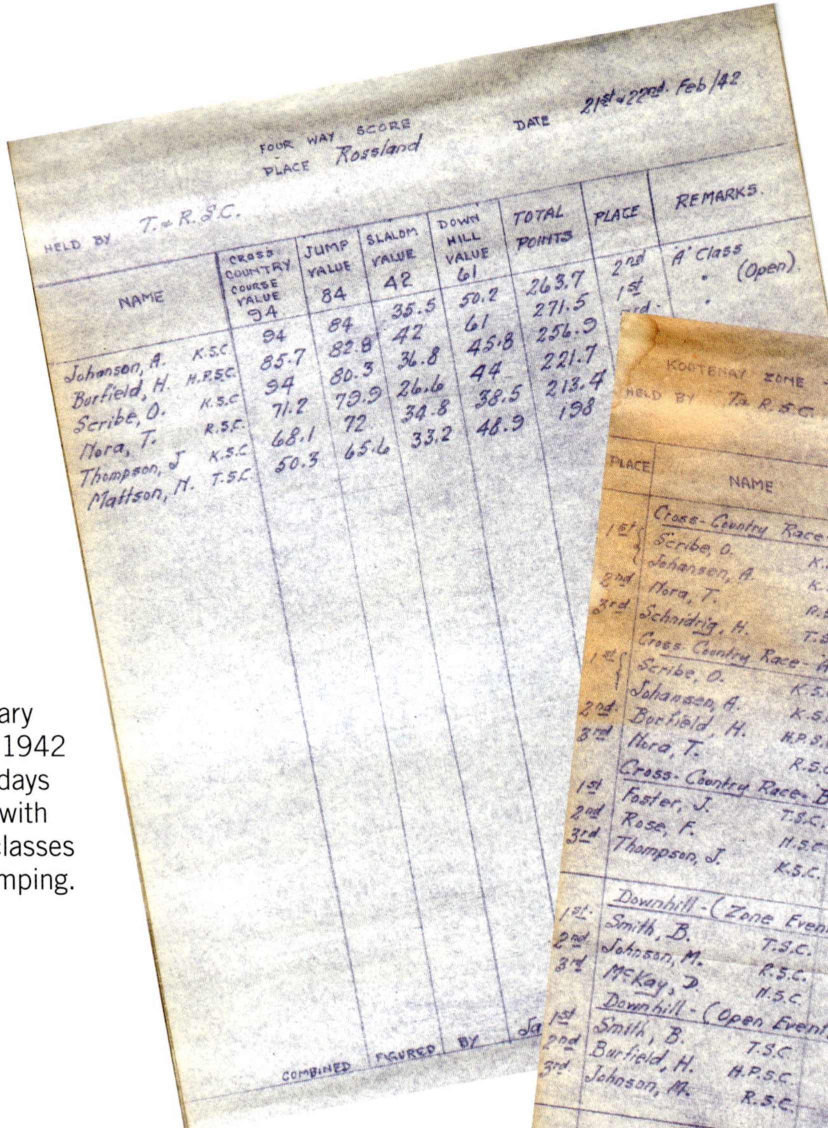

FOUR WAY SCORE
PLACE Rossland
DATE 21st & 22nd Feb /42
HELD BY T. & R.S.C.

NAME	CROSS COUNTRY COURSE VALUE 94	JUMP VALUE 84	SLALOM VALUE 42	DOWN HILL VALUE 61	TOTAL POINTS	PLACE	REMARKS
Johanson, A. K.S.C	94	84	35.5	50.2	263.7	2nd	"A" Class
Burfield, H. H.P.S.C	85.7	82.8	42	61	271.5	1st	" (Open)
Scribe, O. K.S.C	94	80.3	36.8	45.8	256.9	3rd	"
Mora, T. R.S.C	71.2	79.9	26.6	44	221.7		
Thompson, J K.S.C	68.1	72	34.8	38.5	213.4		
Mattson, M. T.S.C	50.3	65.6	33.2	48.9	198		

COMBINED FIGURED BY Ja

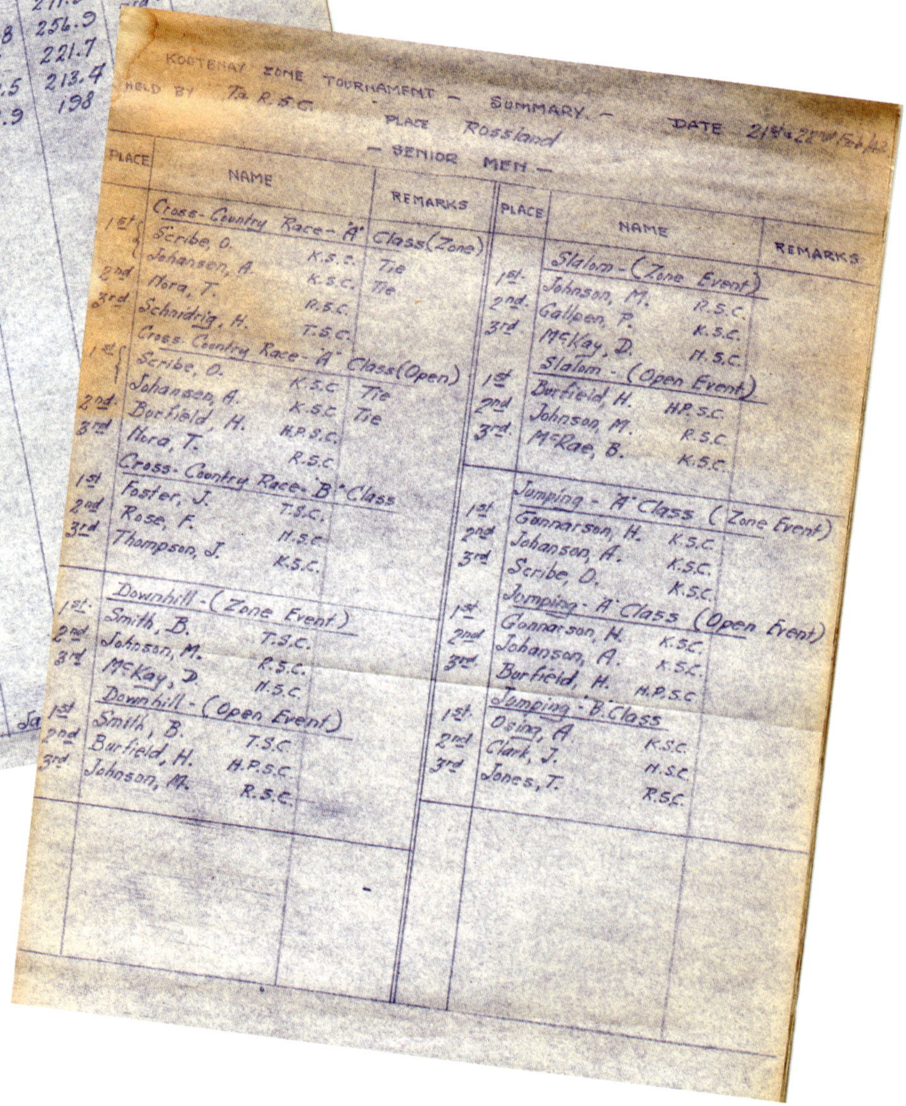

KOOTENAY ZONE TOURNAMENT – SUMMARY – DATE 21st & 22nd Feb /42
HELD BY T. & R.S.C. PLACE Rossland
– SENIOR MEN –

PLACE	NAME		REMARKS
	Cross-Country Race – "A" Class (Zone)		
1st	Scribe, O.	K.S.C.	Tie
	Johansen, A.	K.S.C.	Tie
2nd	Mora, T.	R.S.C.	
3rd	Schneidrig, H.	T.S.C.	
	Cross-Country Race – "A" Class (Open)		
1st	Scribe, O.	K.S.C.	Tie
	Johansen, A.	K.S.C.	Tie
2nd	Burfield, H.	H.P.S.C.	
3rd	Mora, T.	R.S.C.	
	Cross-Country Race – "B" Class		
1st	Foster, J.	T.S.C.	
2nd	Rose, F.	M.S.C.	
3rd	Thompson, J.	K.S.C.	
	Downhill – (Zone Event)		
1st	Smith, B.	T.S.C.	
2nd	Johnson, M.	R.S.C.	
3rd	McKay, D.	M.S.C.	
	Downhill – (Open Event)		
1st	Smith, B.	T.S.C.	
2nd	Burfield, H.	H.P.S.C.	
3rd	Johnson, M.	R.S.C.	

PLACE	NAME		REMARKS
	Slalom – (Zone Event)		
1st	Johnson, M.	R.S.C.	
2nd	Gallpen, P.	K.S.C.	
3rd	McKay, D.	M.S.C.	
	Slalom – (Open Event)		
1st	Burfield, H.	H.P.S.C.	
2nd	Johnson, M.	R.S.C.	
3rd	McRae, B.	K.S.C.	
	Jumping – "A" Class (Zone Event)		
1st	Gonnarson, H.	K.S.C.	
2nd	Johanson, A.	K.S.C.	
3rd	Scribe, O.	K.S.C.	
	Jumping – "A" Class (Open Event)		
1st	Gonnarson, H.	K.S.C.	
2nd	Johanson, A.	K.S.C.	
3rd	Burfield, H.	H.P.S.C.	
	Jumping – "B" Class		
1st	Osing, A.	K.S.C.	
2nd	Clark, J.	M.S.C.	
3rd	Jones, T.	R.S.C.	

JEAN CHALMERS

Housewife Steals Show From Olympic Ski Star

By NANCY WEST

A shy, quiet Vancouver housewife stole the show from an Olympic champion in the annual giant slalom tournament Sunday morning on Grouse Mountain.

Mrs. Walt Chalmers — Jean Chalmers on the entry form — finished 16 seconds behind the day's star, Olympic winner Stein Eriksen, when all times were counted.

Her time of one minute and 40 seconds—an unbelievably fast time for a woman over the prolonged slalom course — earned this slim auburn-haired girl 12th ranking within a field of close to 60 men skiers.

HE'S TOPS

The winner, of course, was Eriksen, a big, blond, Oslo-born champion who is currently conceded one of the best skiers in world competition.

His time for the course was one minute, 24.9 seconds. Runnerup John Frazee of the ex-UBC Thunderbirds Club finished in one minute 34.1 seconds, and Khandar winner Doug Fraser was third in 1:35.2.

The day's jumping honors went again to that Norwegian-born teen-ager Halvar Sellesback, who turned in two of the prettiest jumps in local competition for 200.4 points.

But from the point of view of the fans—2000 of them jammed the race hills—Eriksen was the man of the hour.

FIRST HERE

The good-looking skier who swept the combined slalom and downhill title at the Olympics last year to become first Olympic champion to appear on a Vancouver ski grounds, got top rating from all who watched Sunday's races.

But Ericksen polled highest with femme fans, who voted the blond, wavy-haired, blue-eyed 25-year-old the handsomest visi-r since Philip, Duke of Edin-h.

RESULTS

Giant Slalom

Women — J. Chalmers 1:40, S. Fraser 1:52.5, M. Menzies, 2:06.2, G. Beaton 2:13.1, L. Allen 2:16.5, B. Martin 2:50.4, L. Suttle 2:50.8, J. Silver 2:53.7.

Men—S. Erikson 1:24.9, J. Frazee 1:34.1, D. Fraser 1:35.2, G. Merry 1:35.4, R. McConnell 1:35.8, F. Atkinson 1:36.9, G. Mills 1:37, D. Shore 1:37.6, R. Tonneson and G. Smith 1:38.4, H. Enquist 1:39.3, P. Seaborn 1:39.4, A. McDonald 1:40.6, D. Rokohen 1:40.8, L. Davis 1:41, R. Antille 1:41.4, K. Stangl 1.41.6, R. Turner 1:41.8, N. Welsh and S. Martin 1:43.1, G. Fisher 1:43.5, G. Anderson 1:45, B. Bowtry jr. 1:45.5, B. Irwin 1:45.7, J. Gawthorne 1:47, R. Peers1:47.5, D. Elle 1:48.5, K. McDonald 1:48.6, G. Cowan 1:49, R. Young 1:50.2, H. Rose 1:50.5, H. Abel 1.51.2 (Jr.), K. Edgetveit 1:51.5, J. Cutler 1:52.2, G. Sprang 1:52.6, J. Allbright 1:53.4, A. Teasdale 1:55.3, J. Pendygrasse 1:55.5, D. Smith 1:56.2, W. Chalmers 1:56.6, R. Atkinson 1:56.8, A. J. Bluechell 1:59.6, G. Blackman 2:02.3, C. Wills 2:03, J. Lockhart 2:03.2, G. Hill 2:03:4, P. Duffy 2.041, R. Macrae 2:07.5, R. Hebron 2:08.7 (Jr.), M. Scott 2:11.6, D. Sturgess 2:15.2 (Jr.), D. Whit 2:21.8, T. Laitenen 2:45.2, A. Barry 2:50.1.

Jumping

A Class—H. Sellesback 200.1, T. Hunt 208.4, J. Roocroft 203.9, R. Ulland, Seattle 199.2, F. Pederson, Seattle 190.7, R. Frank 175.2.

B Class — J. Halstead 200.4, C. Montgomery 198.9, R. Ulland, Seattle 194.7, O. Odegaard, Seattle, 186.7, K. Ulland, Seattle 184.8, D. Kleinsorge and W. Thompson 183.5, L. Allen 182.3, K. McDonald 181.3, A. McDonald 180.6, R. Glover 177.3, B. Clarke 176.6, G. Hill 172.9.

Juniors—H. Abel 174.9, R. Ostby 1:63.2.

Seniors—T. Mobraaten 200.1, H. Burfield 183.5, A. Brenner 179, J. Bird, Seattle 178.3.

HOLLYBURN PACIFIC SKI CLUB

MEMBERSHIP CARD

SENIOR

SEASON 1942-43

Name: Harry Burfield

W. J. Macey — PRESIDENT

DATE

Olive Pavey — SECRETARY

I'll bet this ribbon
got some good
laughs!

A handsome group on top of a beautiful mountain. Harry is second from the left.

Harry during training with the RCAF. Mapping coordinates in the aircraft was one of many skills requiring qualification.

23
EFTS
CHAMPIONS

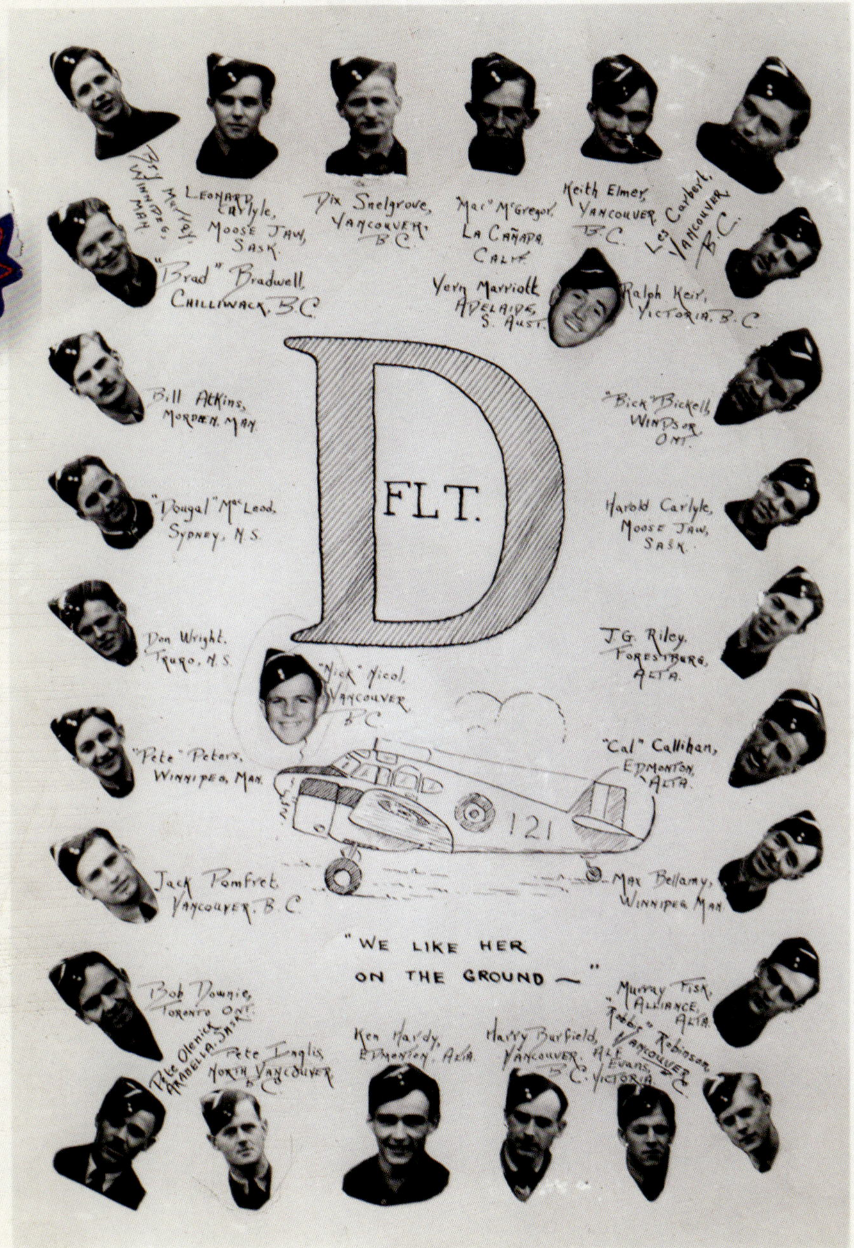
LEONARD CARLYLE, MOOSE JAW, SASK.
DIX SNELGROVE, VANCOUVER, B.C.
"MAC" McGREGOR, LA CAÑADA CALIF.
KEITH ELMER, VANCOUVER B.C.
LES CARBERT, VANCOUVER B.C.
"BRAD" BRADWELL, CHILLIWACK. B.C.
VERN MARRIOTT ADELAIDE, S. AUST.
RALPH KEIR, VICTORIA. B.C.
BILL ATKINS, MORDEN. MAN.
"BICK" BICKELL WINDSOR ONT.
"DOUGAL" McLEOD, SYDNEY, N.S.
D FLT.
HAROLD CARLYLE, MOOSE JAW, SASK.
DON WRIGHT. TRURO, N.S.
J.G. RILEY. FORESTBURG, ALTA.
"NICK" NICOL, VANCOUVER B.C.
"PETE" PETERS, WINNIPEG, MAN.
"CAL" CALLIHAN, EDMONTON, ALTA.
121
JACK POMFRET. VANCOUVER. B.C.
MAX BELLAMY, WINNIPEG MAN.
"WE LIKE HER ON THE GROUND —"
BOB DOWNIE, TORONTO ONT.
MURRAY FISK, ALLIANCE, ALTA.
PETE OLENICK ARABELLA. SASK.
PETE INGLIS NORTH VANCOUVER B.C.
KEN HARDY, EDMONTON, ALTA.
HARRY BURFIELD, VANCOUVER. B.C.
ALF EVANS, VICTORIA
"ROBBY" ROBINSON, VANCOUVER B.C.

Harry ↑

3 SFTS
121
CALGARY

23 EFTS DAVIDSON

Harry in uniform,
1944.

Harry's parents, Emma and Joseph Burfield, 1944.

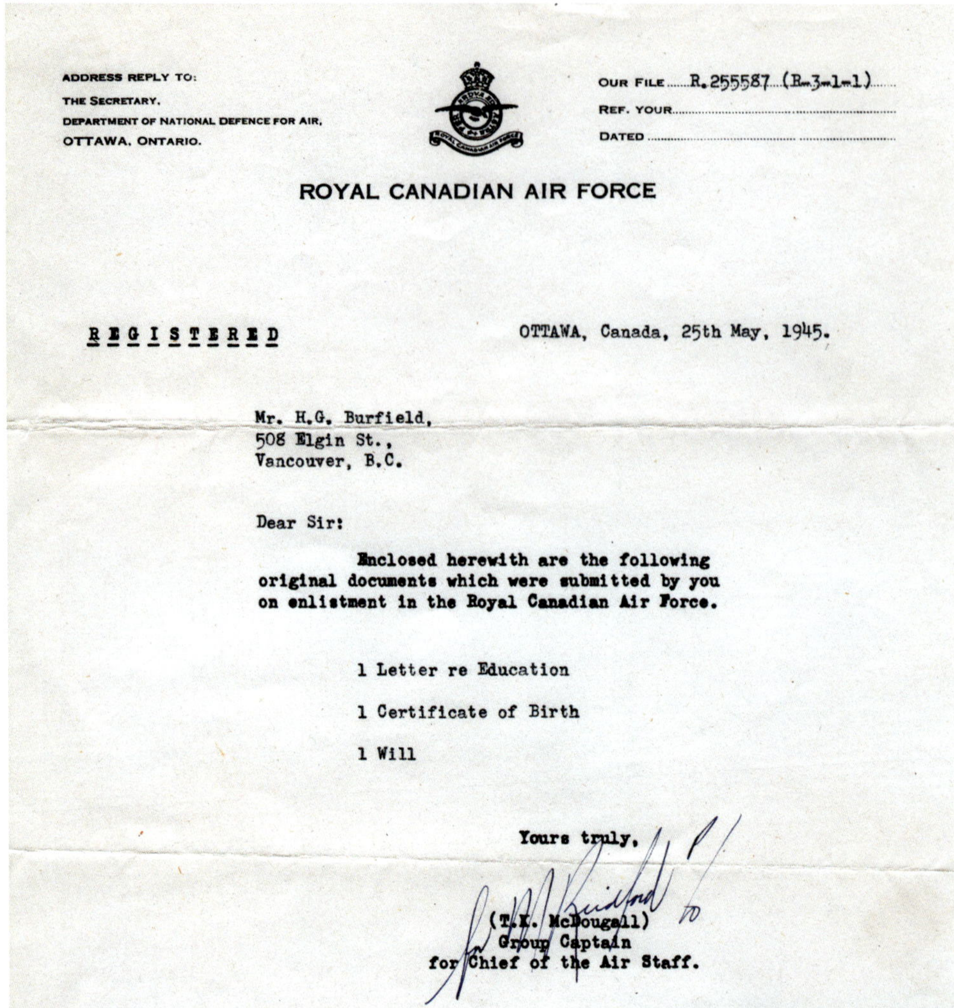

ADDRESS REPLY TO:
THE SECRETARY,
DEPARTMENT OF NATIONAL DEFENCE FOR AIR,
OTTAWA, ONTARIO.

OUR FILE R.255587 (R-3-1-1)
REF. YOUR
DATED

ROYAL CANADIAN AIR FORCE

REGISTERED

OTTAWA, Canada, 25th May, 1945.

Mr. H.G. Burfield,
508 Elgin St.,
Vancouver, B.C.

Dear Sir:

Enclosed herewith are the following original documents which were submitted by you on enlistment in the Royal Canadian Air Force.

1 Letter re Education

1 Certificate of Birth

1 Will

Yours truly,

(T.K. McDougall)
Group Captain
for Chief of the Air Staff.

Letter to Harry from the Royal Canadian Air Force, 1945.

Harry (left) about to receive an award from the Royal Candian Air Force. He graduated one month before the war ended and did not go on any combat missions.

In 1946, the Burfield family purchased the Hollyburn Ski Camp and renamed it Hollyburn Ski Lodge. They made several improvements to accomodate the ever-increasing number of visitors to the mountain.

above: The Burfield family inside the Hollyburn Lodge, 1946. (left to right) Harry, Emma, Joseph, Fred and his wife, Evelyn Kathleen (Evy) Burfield.
source: West Vancouver Archives. Hollyburn Heritage Society Collection. 759.WVA.HHS.BUR

Fred Burfield outside the First Aid cabin at Romstead's on Hollyburn, 1940s.

source: West Vancouver Archives. Hollyburn Heritage Society Collection. 784.WVA.HHS.BUR

Page Three

Noted BC Athletes Awarded Pilot's Wings At Calgary

Vancouver and British Columbia athletes were among graduates of the final class of pilots from No. 3 S.F.T.S., Calgary, recently.

Sgt. J. B. Pomfret, 3731 West Thirteenth, who received his wings, has won five Canadian championships and set one world record in 50-yard breast stroke competition.

Another outstanding swimmer among the graduates is Sgt. R. M. Curry, 1950 Cedar Crest, Canadian junior champion in 1934. He also was a member of the University of British Columbia intercollegiate championship football squad of 1940.

BROTHERS GRADUATE.

Graduating together were two brothers,, Sgt. R. L. Hughes and Sgt. E. L. Hughes of Victoria, each of whom holds three cups for rowing.

Sgt. H. G. Burfield, of Courtenay, Vancouver Island, is an ex-champion skier for western Canada and runnerup in several international skiing tournaments.

Sgt. G. A. Chrisman, speed skater and cyclist, is the son of Mrs. C. T. Chrisman, 2075 West Forty-third. Possessors of several cups for yacht racing are Sgts. D. MacKenzie, 1936 West Seventh, and A. C. Evans, Victoria, while Sgt. D. E. Robinson, 3588 West Twenty-fifth, once set up a provincial high school record for the pole vault.

Another yacht racing expert is Sgt. D. O. Sudbury, 3628 West Third; Sgt. W. R. Snelgrove, Victoria, has medals for marksmanship, and Sgts. L. E. Carbert, 3469 West Forty-second, and J. D. Smith, 196 East King Edward, have trophies for soccer.

Other B.C. airmen among the graduates at Calgary included S. T. Dawes, Penticton; K. S. Elmer, 3216 East Pender; R. D. Keir, Cobble Hill; R. G. Humphreys, Kamloops, son of Dr. F. A. Humphreys, Dominion Government pathologist; P. M. Inglis, 2388 Marine drive, and formerly on the staff of The Vancouver Daily Province; S. G. Nicol, 217 West 19th, whose brother, FO. G. G. Nicol, has been reported missing; J. S. Canham, 1569 West Sixty-fifth; P. G. Guman, ex-football coach, 2980 West Eighth.

J. D. Hannay, Haney; N. E. Andrew, Joyce road; J. M. Mill, New Westminster; H. D. Wey, Cornwall; R. G. Bremner, New Westminster; C. T. Etchell, 4094 West Twelfth; P. J. Fry, Inglewood avenue: A. B. Greig, Penticton; R. Kendall, Kelowna; H. Smith, Rutland; J. Stewart, Kamloops; W. Wilby, Victoria; D. M. Willard, Archimedes, Vancouver.

BURFIELD IN SKI VICTORY

Hollyburn, Vancouver and Seymour Ski Clubs held their club races on Vancouver's favorite mountain ski slopes yesterday.

Harry Burfield topped the cross country plankers for Hollyburn, while Ole Johannesen was the first in the best class of Vancouver Club skiers at Grouse Mountain.

Over on the Seymour ridge young Dorothy Gladstone was the best in the ladies' only downhill event and Walt Richardson took over first place in the men's A class.

Hollyburn Cross Country

"A" Class—Harry Burfield (49.27). "B" Class—J. Wood (53.41), J. Foster (62.52), B. Switzer (66.25). "C" Class—Ted Yard (30.15). Juniors—Paddy Wing (28.19), Jack Roocroft (29.15).

Vancouver Cross Country

"A" Class—O. Johannesen (49.37), M. Swedahl (51.11). B" Class—M. Kraner (53,31), J. Owen (62.20). "C" Class—R. Caverley (31.58). Juniors—A. Teasdale (29.08), D. Manning (31.38), G. Sayce (32.35).

Seymour Downhill

Girls—Dorothy Gladstone (2.05:7). Eda Richardson (2:51:08). Boys "A" Class—Gordie Oran (2:47:3), Bob Townsend (2:50:5), Norm Fairhead (3:03:1), Gordie Bengefield (3:08:6), Chuck Stern (3:54:2), Lorne Eastholm (3:57:5), George Publicover (4:17:4).

MONDAY, FEBRUARY 1, 1943

Irwin Victor In Men's Ski Events

Bill Irwin, flashy ski star of the Irish Fusiliers, led a classy field of downhill and slalom planksters in a clean sweep of the honors in the men's events across the Inlet on Sunday. "Porky" led Harry Burfield and ski-smoothie Stan Tomlinson in the downhill. They were closely followed by Doug Ross, a real up-and-coming skier.

Harry was second to his ski-palsy by only .6 seconds in the slalom. "Spud" Paul, another Amberite, placed third to edge out Bob Sharples and John Cassa.

Joan Cranswick led the fair sex to the finish in the downhill with a 6-second lead over Dot McInnis. Daisy Johnson was third, followed by Jenny Lind.

Daisy reversed the procedure in the slalom by edging Dot McInnis by one second. Dodo Coombie was third.

Although combined results are not as yet available, it seems Joan Cranswick will have the ladies' honor. Her advantage in the downhill appears too strong for Dot McInnis to overcome in the slalom.

Paddy Wing, young Chinese H.P.S.C. ski star, followed in the footsteps of Irwin by winning both events and the combined. Jack Roocroft, H.P.S.C. "wild man," was second in the downhill, followed by Gavin Robinson (another brother Bill). Allan Teasdale was second in the slalom, followed by Jerry Lockhart.

Dave Mathews and Ed Oakley missed the downhill start, but were in there fighting to the finish in the slalom.

Vic Stevens was on hand, but declined to race—first time up the hill in four years for Vic.

DOWNHILL RESULTS.

Junior—1, Paddy Wing, HPSC, 39.6; 2, Jack Roocroft, HPSC, 40.4; 3, Gavin Robinson, Tyee, 44; 4, Pate Robb, VSC, 44.6; 5, Bus Lind, VSC, 48.

Ladies—1, Joan Cranswick, VSC, 118.4; 2, Dot McInnis, Tyee, 124.4; 3, Daisy Johnson, HPSC, 147.2; 4, Jenny Lind, VSC, 149.4; 5, Ruth Baggley, VWSC, 150; 6, Dodo Crombie, VSC, 158.6; 7, Dot Burniston, VSC, 209.4.

Men—1, Bill Irwin, I.F. 1st Battn., 28.6; 2, Harry Burfield, HPSC, 29.2; 3, Spud Paul, Amber, 30.4; 4, Bob Sharples, HPSC, 30.6; Johnny Cassa, Amber, 31.6; Gavin Hyde, VSC, 32; 7, Doug Ross HPSC, 32.6.

SLALOM.

Junior—1, Paddy Wing, HPSC, 35; 2, A. Teasdale, HPSC, 37.8; 3, Gerry Lockhart, VSC, 38.6; 4, Gavin Robinson, Tyee, 39.8.

Ladies—1, Daisy Johnson, HPSC, 37; 2, Dot McInnis, Tyee, 38.2; 3, Dodo Crombie, VSC, 39.6; 4, Joan Cranswick, VSC, 42.2.

Men—1, Bill Irwin, I.F. 1st. Battn.; 2, Harry Burfield, HPSC, 29.2; 3, Spud Paul, Amber, 30.4; 4, Bob Sharples, HPSC, 30.6; 5, Johnny Cassa, Amber, 31.6; 6, Gavin Hyde, VSC, 32; 7, Doug Ross, HPSC, 32.6.

FLIES HIGH—Bill Irwin, high-flying ski star from Princeton, who is now a fully paid-up member of the Irish Fusiliers, is pictured here in characteristic pose. Bill cleaned up in Sunday's ski tourney across the Inlet.

TOO MUCH ICE

Bill Irwin Smashes Record Winning Viskie Ski Classic

Bill Irwin, Irish Fusiliers "Ski Demon," led a flashy field in the Viskie classic on Sunday to add another title to his long list. In winning he smashed the old record make by Druce Cooke of 6:46. "Porky" ran the course in the remarkable time of 6:13 to lead Harry Burfield, who also slaughtered the previous time by 15 seconds.

Solid ice over the entire length of the two-mile route forced the officials to cancel the ladies' event, and added to the difficulties the lads had in running the course. The fact that it was as hard as concrete enabled the racers to make good time over the bottom cross-country part though they were a tired lot at the finish.

Jack Pratt turned in a very good run of 6:49.4, despite the fact he lost a ski pole, to anchor third spot.

He beat Ernie Griffiths who was followed by George Robinson.

Irwin was the only racer who didn't spill on the icy surface. Harry Burfield had one sitzmark but didn't lose much time. Most of the other "langlaufers" caught their skis in the icy ruts and have many a bruise to display.

Results:

1, Bill Irwin, Irish Fusiliers, 6:13.4; 2, Harry Burfield, H.P.S.C., 6:28.4; 3, Jack Pratt (FIS) H.P.S.C., 6:49.4; 4, Ernie Griffiths, Tyee, 7:08.8; 5, George Robinson, H.P.S.C., 7:11.8; Art Johnson, V.S.C., 7:12.4; 6, Ole Johannsen, V.S.C., 7:15; 7, Henry Setvedt, V.S.C., 7:15.8; 8, Karl Baadsvick, Tyee, 7:29.8; 9, Ed Oakley, H.P.S.C., 7:49; 10, Stan Body, G.M.S.C., 7:52.4; 11, Bob Crosby, U.B.C., 7:56.

Harry enjoying another great day in flight on Hollyburn Mountain. The jumps were recorded by the men standing on the side-lines. They would run out after the jumpers had landed and mark out the landing points using ski poles.

In those early days, there were no roads or any other means to get supplies up the mountain. People had to pack heavy loads on their backs, including supplies to build cabins. Fred was offered this machine for $100. It was supposed to make access to Hollyburn easier. It didn't work so he didn't end up paying. To this day, visitors to the mountain have to hike in. Many see this as an important part of the heritage of visiting Hollyburn Mountain.

Harry and other ski jumpers of the time were always pushing the boundaries of the sport by trying flips and other acrobatics. Sometimes they didn't complete their flips which would be evident by the snow on their backs. Their skis were up to 7' long (213.36 cm). These postcards were used to promote Hollyburn Mountain.

"Ski Acrobats" - Hollyburn Ridge

Postcards of Harry on Hollyburn mountain.

"On the Peak of Hollyburn"

"On Hollyburn Peak"

"Vancouver Ski Club Cabin" - Hollyburn Ridge

"Looking over Vancouver towards Mt. Baker" - from Hollyburn

Pool Ski Meet Thrills Thousands

DARING TANDEM JUMP on the narrow ski "hill" at Kitsilano Beach was a feature of Saturday's spectacle there. Larry Allen and Art Menzies gave the crowd a thrill as they roared down the runway together.

Snow, Water Sports on Same Program

Vancouver, with some of the continent's best skiing grounds on its doorstep, had a full-scale ski jumping meet right in its living room, Saturday.

More than 7000 persons swarmed over the lawns adjoining Kitsilano pool to witness the opening of Evergreen Hill which was promptly folded up again after the crowd-thrilling spectacle was ended.

By way of boasting about Vancouver's versatility as a playground, swimmers cavorted in the pool and water skiers and yachts slid over the waters of English Bay, a snowball's toss away.

The spectacle was sponsored by The Vancouver Sun and the Junior Chamber of Commerce.

FLAMING TORCHES

Everybody liked the show so much it was repeated again Saturday night when the skiers added an extra thrill by going over the jump with flaming torches in their hands.

Harry Burfield of Vancouver Ski Club was the meet champion and sailed off with the perpetual Eiler's Jewelry Trophy.

The contest produced probably the shortest ski jump records in the world but it had all the appeal of a real mountain-top leap.

In the afternoon, 54 feet was the longest jump but later, when the sun and the wind went down, the hill speeded up and the boys were soaring to 80 feet from the take-off.

MELTING SLOWED

Fifty feet high and 175 feet long, the tubular-steel structure, covered with wooden planking, was packed hard with crushed ice. Snow cement, a special chemical, slowed up the melting process under a hot sun.

Some of the jumpers came down on the seat of their slacks instead of their skis but there were no accidents. Larry Allen and Art Menzies almost went over the side into the crowd when they performed a side-by-side leap.

The boys roared down the four-foot wide jump together. As they zoomed into the air their flailing arms collided and both wobbled dangerously in mid-air. But they made it.

TRAPEZE ACT

Runners-up to Burfield in "A" class were Henry Sotvedt and Ole Johanson. Jim Henniger took first place in "B" class, followed by Al Menzies and Dick Lyons.

Pick of the juniors was Halvor Sellesback with Dick Anderson second and Ted Hunt third. First place skiers in all classes were Vancouver Ski Club members.

MArine 1161

Winter Sport Vies

SKI-JUMPING AND SWIMMING, a snowball's throw apart, featured a show that drew 7000 to Kitsilano Beach

Saturday ing the

Courtesy of The Vancouver Sun

The Vancouver Sun

VANCOUVER, BRITISH COLUMBIA, MONDAY, MAY 8, 1950

Swimming at Kitsilano Beach Spectacle, Saturday Afternoon

... This is part of the crowd witness-
...ng from a 50-foot-high steel jump erected on the lawns fronting the beach. The run was covered with crushed ice. Hardy bathers disported in the pool nearby. The spectacle was sponsored by The Vancouver Sun and Junior Chamber of Commerce.

Skiers Hold Frolic By Kitsilano Pool

By PETER SPRING

The mountain came to the ski jumpers Saturday when a 60-foot tubular steel ski jump was constructed in conjunction with the Kitsilano sports show for tourist promotion at the Kitsilano Pool.

Harry Burfield of the Vancouver Ski Club won the Eilers Ltd. trophy for A class jumping with 201.2 points.

Runnerup, Henry Sotvedt, also of the Vancouver Ski Club, was only one-tenth of a point behind Burfield. Ole Johanson, forestry supervisor on Mount Seymour was third with 195.2 points.

Jim Hennager, Vancouver Ski Club, thrilled over 5000 persons in taking honors in the B class with 198.6 points.

Al Menzies placed second in the same event with 197.6 points and Dick Lyons third with 190.4 points.

Junior skiers outdid themselves in the person of Halvar Sellesback, young Norwegian leaper now skiing for the Vancouver Ski Club. Sellesback made the highest total score of the meet with 202.4 points.

Dick Anderson was second with 191 points and Ted Hunt third with 180.7 points and a fall.

Exhibition ski jumping took place in the evening and was concluded by flaming torches being carried by skiers as they leaped over the jump. Flaming straw was placed at the top of the landing hill and jumpers leaped through the flames.

Canadian Ski Patrol was on hand at all times to control the crowd and attend to safety of the jumpers.

Here are the results:

A Class men: H. Burfield 201.2, H. Sotvedt 201.1; O. Johanson 195.2, J. Woods 189.9, A. Johannson 180.9, M. Swedahl 175.5.

B Class men: J. Hennager 198.6, A. Menzies 197.6, D. Lyons 190.4, A. MacDonald 185.9, E. Marwick 184.9, R. Glover 184.7, W. Thompson 183.2, G. Samson 180.9, R. DesHarnais 178.1, K. MacDonald 172.1, L. Allen 170, B. Clarke 164.7.

Junior class: H. Sellesback 202.4, Anderson 191, T. Hunt 180.7, D. 144.3.

"STUMP JUMPERS."—First of their kind to brave the stump Hollyburn trails for an early ski inspection of the Ridge. Reading from the left: Bud James, Olav Ulland of Norway, Jack Pratt and Harry Burfield caught near Hollyburn Peak in about two feet of snow.

There Is Snow on the Hills But Ski Sport Is Only Fair

By DON TYRELL.

Impatient Hollyburn Ridge skiers stole a march on their less fortunate brethren last Wednesday, when Harry Burfield, Bud James and Jack Pratt of the Hollyburn Pacific Ski Club conducted Olav Ulland, famed Norwegian ski jumper, over the Ridge. Joan Mathews, probably the first girl to ski on the Ridge this season, says the snow was good and powdery with only a slight crust on top.

The treeless parts of the Shoulder made good going but the rest of the party's ski-ing consisted mainly of early season "stump jumping." Old skis were worn the better to withstand scrapings of the thinly covered blueberry bushes and stumps. Ski-ing on the Ridge at present is not safe and great care must be used to avoid bruising the more tender parts of the anatomy on rocks and frozen ground.

Temperature at Hollyburn Ski Camp at 8 o'clock last night was 18 above with the thermometer definitely on the downgrade. Oscar Pearson reports good skating.

"Hollyburn Ski Lodge"

"LITTLE SUN VALLEY"

Great Plans On Hollyburn

By PETER SPRING

Hollyburn Ridge will resemble a "Little Sun Valley" before very long if sprucing up plans of the Hollyburn Ridge Administrative committee fall into place during the next few months.

The committee is an unofficial body chosen by the West Vancouver Municipal council at a special meeting Wednesday to map plans for orderly development, coinciding with construction of the New Hollyburn Aerial Tram.

Fire prevention, sanitation, construction, ski trails, ski patrol activities and future development of ski facilities were all discussed.

READY SITE

Progress of Hollyburn ski lift was reported by President Roy C. Sims, who said cutting of the right of way was complete to the "Forks" and loggers were readying the site for the large ski lodge terminal. Concrete has been poured for eight of the large steel towers and a coffee shop will soon be completed at the bottom terminal.

The proposed Hollyburn ski jump, possibly Revelstoke's closest rival, came one step nearer when Vancouver Ski Club sports chairman, Les May, displayed the blueprint profile of the proposed structure. The Vancouver Ski Club has been producing large numbers of ski jumpers for many years and with a jump as big as they plan, Vancouver jumpers could lead in Canada.

Theme of the informal meeting was one of complete cooperation and sound planning for future skiers and sport enthusiasts.

Vancouver Junior Chamber of Commerce, which organized the recent ski jumping at Kitsilano, outlined plans to continue their work on local slopes.

* * *

Sandra Tomlinson, Vancouver's lady of the skis, is now in California at the famous Norden Sugar Bowl. Sandra has been working at Sun Valley and Squaw Valley, as well as skiing in many major American and international races.

The Portland Golden Rose Festival ski tourney on Mount Hood, June 11, will attract a number of Vancouver ski stars as well as Sandra. Sister Barbara hopes to capture the traveling Miss and bring her home, although several of Sandra's international ski fans are talking of Switzerland.

Skiing at Mount Baker is perfect these days with over 15 feet at the lodge and more at Austin Pass. Ski tows run weekends and the main lodge is closed until the Heather Cup Giant Slalom and Thundermug jump meet, July 4.

Harry Burfield captured the combined title for B Class skiers after finishing first in the cross-country and sixth in the jumping. Bill Bourne, who won the jumping event in the class in the afternoon had had an indifferent showing in the racing and fell back to third in the combined, allowing George Robinson, who finished third in the jumps and well up in the racing, to capture second place in the combined event.

Vancouver Picks Up Four Firsts; Burfield, Fiddler Score

When Tom Mobraaten arrives in Washington this weekend to meet some of the world's best skiers he will pack along the city jumping, cross country and combined titles with him. The smiling Norwegian lad, fresh from brilliant performances at Banff, was right in his glory on Hollyburn Ridge yesterday.

Mobraaten captured the jumping with a point total of 149.21. He did not find it easy winning the leap, however, Ole Svedahl, fellow Vancouver Ski Clubber, winding up in second place just one-tenth of a point behind Tom.

Einar Ellingruud, good looking Hollyburn Pacific Ski Club jumper, captured third place, with Earl Young, Nels Nelsen and Stan Laurensen of the "Viskies" following in that order. Ellingruud was the only H. P. S. C. skier to show anything in this event.

BOURNE WINS

Competition was exceedingly close in the "B" and "C" class jumping. Bill Bourne of Hollyburn won "B" class, with Jack Abrams of Vancouver second and George Robinson of Hollyburn third. John Shaw of Vancouver captured "C" class honors, with Norm Fiddler second and Jack Wood third. The latter two are Hollyburners.

Mobraaten won the cross-country event quite handily. He finished the course in 36 minutes and 41 seconds. Gus Johnson, one of the best cross-country men in Canada, was second. The Hollyburn ace, who has been slowed up all season with injuries, crossed the line in 38 minutes and 11 seconds. Bran Muir of the "Viskies" was third, just four seconds behind Johnson.

The "B" class boys hit quite a clip, with Hollyburn copping top place. Harry Burfield was the winner in 39 minutes and 35 seconds. Bill Sutherland of Hollyburn was second, and Syd Smith of Vancouver third. Burfield won the "B" class combined.

G[illegible] TOMORROW

Bud James showed his heels to his fellow "C" class cross-country racers, winning in 19 minutes and 20 seconds. Norm Fiddler and Vic Stevens followed him in that order. Stevens was only four seconds behind second-place Fiddler. The latter won the "C" class combined.

The weather was fair for the first day's city championship events. Rain fell in the morning for a while, but in the afternoon the clouds disappeared.

A large crowd is expected to climb Grouse Mountain today and tomorrow to witness the men's and women's downhill and slalom city championship events. More than 100 entries have been received for this event.

RESULTS

Class "A" jumping — 1, Mobraaten, 149.2; 2, Ole Svedahl, 1.49.1; 3, Ellingruud, 1.45.4; 4, E. Young, 1.38.6; 5, Nels Nelsen, 1.36.5; 6, S. Laurenson, 88.8.

Class "B" jumping—Bill Bourne, 1.44; 2, Jack Abrams, 1.40.1; 3, George Robinson, 1.35.4.

Class "C" jumping—1, John Shaw, 1.39.2; 2, Norm Fiddler, 1.25.8; 3, Jack Wood, 1.21.7.

Junior jumping—1, Glen McDonald, 1.29.5; 2, Jack Pratt, 1.04.5; 3, Russ White, 92.5.

Class "A" cross country—T. Mobraaten, 36.41; 2, Gus Johnson, 38.11; 3, Bruan Muir, 38.15.

Class "B" cross country—H. Burfield, 39.35; 2, Bill Sutherland, 40.07; 3, Syd Smith, 40.11.

Class "C" cross country—1, Bud James, 19.20; 2, Norm Fiddler, 21.04; 3, Vic Stevens, 21.08.

COMBINED CHAMPIONS

Class "A"—Tom Mobraaten.
Class "B"—H. Burfield.
Class "C"—Nor. Fiddler.
Juniors—Jack Pratt.

Harry and the other members of the Hollyburn Pacific Ski Club wore red sweaters made by Evelyn Burfield. She was a great seamstress and often made clothes for her family.

Ski Heil!

Burfield Wins Downhill Race

Harry Burfield topped a classy field in a wild race through yesterday's snowstorm, to win the Hollyburn Pacific Ski Club downhill championship test from Hollyburn Peak in one minute 17 seconds. Art Hullah, skiing for the Vancouver Ski Slub over the same course, led his gang home but was eight seconds off Burfield's time.

Two Viskies finished immediately behind Hullah, Brian Creer coming in with 1:30 and Ed Richardson making the trip in 1:34. Bob Sharples was the second Hollyburn member to finish. His time was the same as Richardson's. Robbie Robinson was third in the Hollyburn.

Joan Cranswick, Vancouver Ski Club, was the best of the "A" class girls, turning a time of 1:46 for the same distance as the men. Ruth Larsen placed second and Nan Roberts, third. Daisy Johnson was the only Hollyburn girl to race "A" class.

Gordon Hall captured first place in the Vancouver Ski Club "B" division while L. Harper performed the same feat in the Hollyburn section. First Viskie junior to finish was Gerry Lockhart while George Nash topped the Hollyburn kids.

Bea McIntosh made the best time in the Hollyburn girls' "B" bracket while Dot Burniston was the fastest of the Viskies.

Burfield Captures Hollyburn-Pacific Downhill Ski Race

Hurtling down from the peak of Hollyburn to the foot of Romstad in 1 minute, 59 seconds, Harry Burfield captured the Hollyburn Pacific Ski Club's downhill race Sunday. Close behind came the pack of the club's Banff team. "Irish" Beaumont was second and "Ace" Lindsay and Bill Brown finished third and fourth respectively.

Norm Fiddler captured the B class race from the Shoulder in 1 minute 23 seconds to nose out Jack Pratt and Stan Harrison.

Margaret Gale, of marathon fame, stepped her way to victory over Tess Murby and Jean McCurdy in the women's event. Miss Gale's time was 1 minute 46 seconds.

More than two hundred attended the club dance Saturday to hono the team for Banff.

Hollyburn Pacific Ski Club's team for this year's Noseeums Kandahar will be **Gus Johnson,** captain; **George Bury, Harry Burfield** and **Kon Lien. Gus,** a veteran downhill racer, is a greatly improved skier this year, according to some of the boys who have been watching him.

Bury made the fastest time of his team in the first two races and will be out to repeat this year. **Harry Burfield,** a coming four-way star, and **Lien,** who hails from Wells, are more than capable of holding up their end up on this well-balanced team.

Wells trophy won by Harry in 1942.

VISKIE CLASSIC

H. Burfield Finishes First Ahead of Champ Bill Irwin

Harry Burfield won the toughest ski race of the season on Hollyburn Ridge yesterday. He topped a classy field of 54 entries to finish first in the fifth annual running of the "Viskie Classic."

One of the best all-round skiers in Canada, Harry negotiated the combination downhill and cross-country course in 7 minutes 42 seconds. Heavy snow conditions hampered the racers and made faster times impossible. It was Harry's second win of the Viskie trophy.

Bill Irwin, visiting stylist from Princeton's Amber Ski Club and Pacific Northwest cross-country and jumping champ, was second to Burfield. Ole Johansen, last year's winner, finished third.

Other racers to wind up near the top were Brian Creer, fourth, Gus Johnson, fifth, Henry Sotvedt, sixth, and Ernie Griffith, seventh. Griffith's showing was particularly good, as he is only recently up from junior ranks and has had little cross-country experience.

Daisy Johnson, who has made winning this race almost a habit, copped the women's silverware for the third time. She was clocked in 10.18. If Daisy wins next year it will be three in a row for her, and she keeps the silverware.

Nancy Roberts took second place, while third position went to Doreen Crombie of the Edmonton Ski Club. Thelma Hutchinson, former Vancouverite now ski-ing for the Nelson Ski Club, placed fourth.

SKI-TOW

SKI-LODGE
HOLLYBURN RIDGE

Mobraaten Wins Jump Title, Ellingrud First In Combined

By DON TYRELL

Tom Mobraaten, Vancouver Ski Club's Pacific Northwest ski jumping champion, gave his fellow townsman a treat on Hollyburn Ridge when he won the Vancouver City ski jumping title on the hill named for him in 1936. Two jumps of 125 and 121 feet in perfect style put Mobraaten ten points ahead of second place Bill Bourne of the Hollyburn Pacific Ski Club.

In addition to having the best form, Mobraaten also had the longest standing jump, 125 feet. Apart from Mobraaten's first and the performance of the young Tyeee ski runner's jumpers in the junior events, the first day of the three-day tourney was dominated by the jumpers and langlaufers of the Hollyburn Pacific.

Einar Ellingrud, with his victory in the A class cross-country and third place in the jumping, won the A combined for Hollyburn. His time for the eight-mile dash was 57.32. Following close on his heels came his fellow club members, George Bury and Kon Lien, to cinch the first three spots in the senior racing division.

Through the efforts of Bud James the Hollyburners earned first place in B class cross-country, while Al Robb placed first in C division racing and third in the jumping to win the combined title in his class.

Harry Burfield, in the B class; Ernie Zellweger in C class, brought in two more firsts in the jumping, and Jack Pratt waltzed away with the junior cross-country to complete the rout for the Hollyburn Club.

Only in the junior jumping division were the Ridgement taken. Five entries from the Tyee Ski Runners turned in an exhibition worthy of good B jumpers to take the first five places. These youngsters, Bill Robinson, Bert Ross, Harold Smithers, Jack Gehrke and Gerald Everell, have the makings of high-class jumpers.

Lew Davis is favored for the downhill and slalom events Sunday on Hollyburn.

How They Finished

Cross-Country.

A class — E. Ellingrud, H.P.S.C., 57.32; G. Bury, H.P.S.C., 60.15; K. Lien, H.P.S.C., 60.50; B. Muir, V.S.C., 69.59; M. Swedahl, V.S.C., 67.59.

B class—B. James, H.P.S.C., 57.47; P. Craft, Wells, 60.46; H. Hyde, V.S.C., 63.11; G. Hyde, V.S.C., 63.15; S. Body, G.M.S.C., 63.45; V. Stevens, V.S.C., 64.47; H. Burfield, H.P.S.C., 65.40; J. Shaw, V.S.C., 67.59; L. May, V.S.C., 70.15; H. Nelson, Wells, 71.26.

C class—A. Robb, H.P.S.C., 29.55; S. Harrison, H.P.S.C., 30.58; E. Zwelleger, H.P.S.C., 31.16; J. Gibson, H.P.S.C., 32.25; J. Perry, H.P.S.C., 32.40; D. Dewar, H.P.S.C., 32.55; H. Aikens, H.P.S.C., 35.35; F. Cotton, T.S.R., 39.58.

Juniors—J. Pratt, H.P.S.C., 28.52; B. Irwin, Amber, 29.03; E. Barker, V.S.C., 32.16; R. Stevens, V.S.C., 32.17; W. Hodson, V.S.C., 34.03; G. Easthom, Mt. S.S.C., 34.58; D. Swanson, H.P.S.C. 37.08.

Jumping.

A class—T. Mobraaten, V.S.C., 236.88; B. Bourne, H.P.S.C., 226.42; E. Ellingrud, H.P.S.C., 206.36; K. Hegseth, H.P.S.C., 206.48; F. Finckenhagen, V.S.C., 178.12; J. Abramson, V.S.C., 143.48; M. Swedahl, V.S.C., 109.84; H. Brown, Pioneer, 94.76.

B class — H. Burfield, H.P.S.C., 213.83; B. Irwin, Amber, 207.02; J. Shaw, V.S.C., 206.78; M. Maki, V.S.C., 206.64; V. Stevens, V.S.C., 197.58; P. Craft, Wells, 196.72; J. Pratt, H.P.S.C., 190.04; H. Nelson, Wells, 184.98; G. Bury, H.P.S.C., 180.68; J. Thompson, Wells, 166.04; L. May, V.S.C., 128.92; B. James, H.P.S.C., 119.36.

C class—E. Zwelleger, H.P.S.C., 195; R. Stevens, V.S.C., 191.5; A. Robb, H.P.S.C., 190.8; S. Harrison, H.P.S.C., 181; C. Ross, V.S.C., 147.8; B. Stevens, T.S.R., 137.8.

Juniors—B. Robinson, T.S.R., 223.3; B. Ross, T.S.R., 209.2; H. Smithers, T.S.R., 204.7; J. Gehrke, T.S.R., 197.6; G. Everell, T.S.R., 170.5; W. Hodson, V.S.C., 152.4; R. Hodson, V.S.C., 150.8; D. Swanson, H.P.S.C., 109.9.

Combined Cross-country and Jumping.

A class—E. Ellingrud, H.P.S.C.; M. Swedahl, V.S.C.

B class—Paul Craft, Wells; H. Burfield, H.P.S.C.; V. Stevens, V.S.C.; J. Shaw, V.S.C.

C class—A. Robb, H.P.S.C.; E. Zwelleger, H.P.S.C.; S. Harrison, H.P.S.C.

Juniors — W. Hodson, V.S.C.; D. Swanson, H.P.S.C.; R. Hodson, V.S.C.

FORMER LOCAL SKIERS COMPETING FROM OTHER POINTS

Revelstoke's Fame As Producing Ground For Expert Skiers Indicated When Former Local Products Carry Outside Colors.

Although Revelstoke ski club will be well represented at the big tournament now in progress, local interest will be extended to embrace a number of former local jumpers who are carrying the colors of other clubs.

These competitors, trained on local hills and most of them native sons, have continued the skisport interest they acquired here, in the communities they now inhabit.

Foremost among the former luminaries is Nels Nelsen, whose name has been synonymous with skiing in Revelstoke for a quarter of a century. Nels is entered from Vancouver but will no doubt take a fatherly interest in the Kamloops entries as he has done a great deal toward making Kamloops skisport conscience, this winter.

Ivind Nelsen, for many years a local star and ski instructor at the Chateau Frontenac, Quebec, will give Kamloops more than an outside chance to get in on the major honors of the tournament.

Another Kamloops entry, representing the Hub City in B class, is Al Norberg, captain of the Kamloops ski club. Al has been a government employee at Kamloops and the Cariboo since he left Revelstoke but he has never lost the inclination to emulate the progress of skiing in Revelstoke, in which he shared as a youngster.

(Continued on page six)

Former Local Skiers

(Continued from Page One)

Harry Burfield, representing the Hollyburn club has been here for over a week and the loss of a pair of skis hasn't dampened his desire to place well up to B class. Harry follows the avocation of a carpenter in Vancouver. As will be remembered Harry's father, J. H. Burfield, was agent for the Canadian Pacific Express Co., here for many years.

Bill Bourne also carries a Vancouver standard in the tournament. Bill hasn't been away from Revelstoke long enough to be forgotten. Formerly one of Revelstoke's best 'B' class jumpers, Bill has graduated to 'A' class since he left Revelstoke.

John Shaw, whose father, J. F. Shaw, was an ardent winter sports fan, during his residence here as manager of the Bank of Montreal, represents the Vancouver ski club in B class. John took to the "slabs" at Revelstoke as a very wee lad, and his progress in the years since, has been marked.

Revelstoke fans need no introduction to Lloyd Bennison, who comes from Copper Mountain to uphold the mining town's reputation at the big tournament. He is an 'A' class jumper, whose consistent good form and distance, was a feature of local tournaments for many years.

Several other former Revelstoke jumpers were expected to be present including Nip Stone and the Manley boys, but the entry list closed without the inclusion of their names.

Among the large attendance from outside points will be quite a number of former Revelstokians, who were in one way or other, connected with earlier Revelstoke tournaments.

NINETY SKI RUNNERS IN "VISKIE CLASSIC"

Twenty - five Americans To Race Sunday.

Ninety skiers will hurtle down Hollyburn Peak's tortuous course Sunday and pole till arm-weary for First Lake Ski Camp in second running of the exacting "Viskie Classic."

That number filed entries Thursday night with Hollyburn Ski Promotion Committee, from fifty "A" Class men, twenty-seven "B" Class men and thirteen "A" Class girls, including twenty-five entrants from below the line.

Girls will (the first time they have had a similar break) lead off at noon in their race for the Rob Roy Trophy held by Daisy Bourdon, H.P.S.C. The defender and Dorothy Hoyt and Virginia Bowden of Washington Ski Club are likely to have a nip-and-tuck fight.

The tough "A" Class grind for the Crystal Finish Trophy will get underway at 12:25 when "Chuck" Gillespie, V.S.C. dips his skis downhill. Favorites are narrowed to Carl Neu of Washington University; Harry Burfield, H.P.S.C.; Konrad Lien, H.P.S.C., and Stan Body, G.M.S.C.

Four medals will be contested for when "B" Class racers are led off by "Sonny" Ross, Viskie, at 1:26. Ross, Frank Featherston and Ed Richardson, V.S.C.; Bud James, Geoff Owen-Jones and Norm Fiddler, H.P.S.C.; and A. Harrington, G.M.S.C. are listed as g contenders.

Harry and his father at Hollyburn. The snow often covered the entire cabin with only the chimney sticking out. They had to dig their way into the cabins after a heavy snowfall!

Harry Filion, Mr & Mrs Gerry Everell, Jim Craig, Harry Burfield, Jack Scott, and Eric Taurillard in front Garibaldi Mountian Chalets, Squamish, BC. (Diamond Head Chalet)

Harry leaning on the hood, always ready to go skiing with poles and skis tied to his car.

Fred Burfield towing members of the West Vancouver Council, 1950s.
source: West Vancouver Archives. Hollyburn Heritage Society Collection. 929.WVAHHS.COL

Chapter Four

A New Generation on Hollyburn Mountain

In 1949 Harry met Katherine "Rene" Ann Morrison. They were married on October 29, 1951 and moved to Hollyburn Mountain. Soon afterwards they started a family. Their son, Richard Joseph Burfield, was born October 3, 1952 and their daughter, Marion Ann Burfield, was born June 2, 1955. During this time Harry still competed in many ski races and jumping competitions.

In 1952 Harry's brother, Fred, and his wife Evelyn "Evy" moved into the Hollyburn Ski Lodge and Harry moved his ski shop to the top of the chair lift at Highview.

After their father's death in 1953, Harry and Fred inherited the Hollyburn Ski Lodge. Harry's family lived on Hollyburn Mountain until 1959 when they moved to North Vancouver.

facing page: Harry and Rene on Granville Street, Vancouver, BC.

The necktie Rene embroidered for Harry.

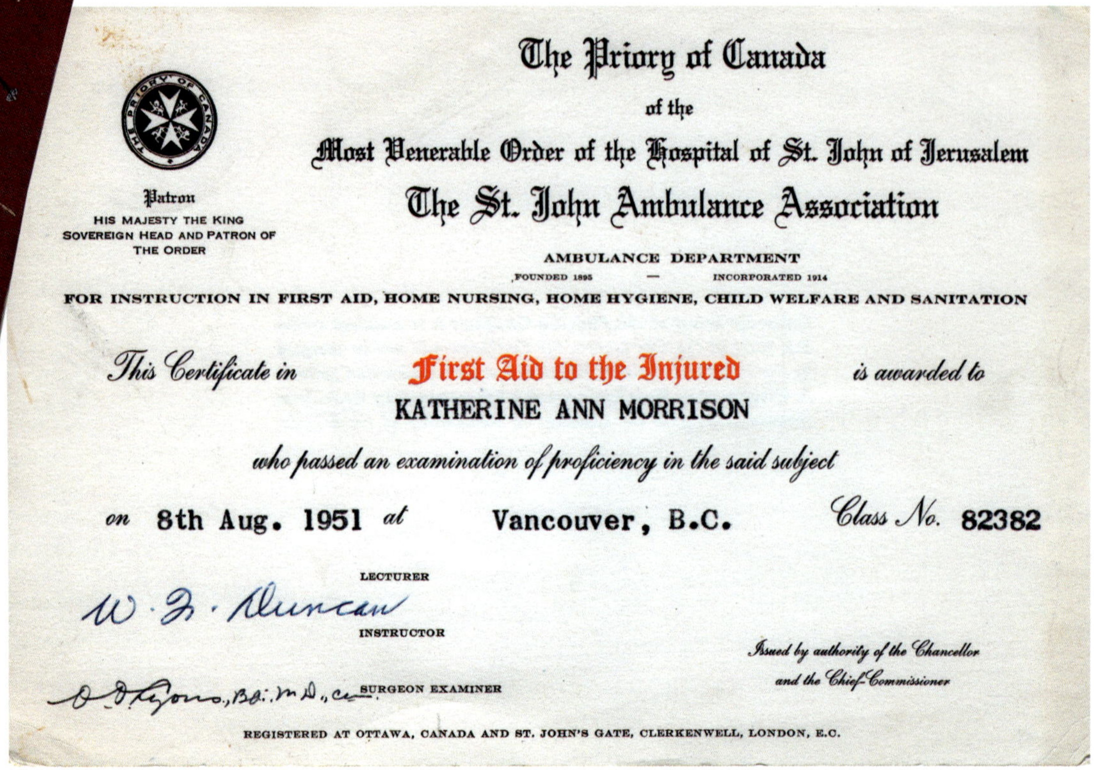

The Priory of Canada

of the

Most Venerable Order of the Hospital of St. John of Jerusalem

The St. John Ambulance Association

Patron
HIS MAJESTY THE KING
SOVEREIGN HEAD AND PATRON OF THE ORDER

AMBULANCE DEPARTMENT

FOUNDED 1895 — INCORPORATED 1914

FOR INSTRUCTION IN FIRST AID, HOME NURSING, HOME HYGIENE, CHILD WELFARE AND SANITATION

This Certificate in **First Aid to the Injured** *is awarded to*

KATHERINE ANN MORRISON

who passed an examination of proficiency in the said subject

on 8th Aug. 1951 *at* Vancouver, B.C. *Class No.* 82382

LECTURER

INSTRUCTOR

SURGEON EXAMINER

Issued by authority of the Chancellor and the Chief Commissioner

REGISTERED AT OTTAWA, CANADA AND ST. JOHN'S GATE, CLERKENWELL, LONDON, E.C.

Rene and Harry both felt it was important to have their First Aid Certificates. They always wanted to be prepared in case of an emergency, especially since they spent so much time out of doors.

Harry and Rene on their wedding day in Vancouver, October 29, 1951. Attending their wedding were Harry's parents, Joseph and Emma Burfield (left) and Rene's mother, Mrs. Kay Morrison-Adams (second from right) and Rene's step father, Brian Adams (right).

Harry getting ready to go spring skiing at the top of Garibaldi Mountain, 1950s. As some still do today, they used to dab warm wax onto the bottom of their skis and use a scraper to spread the wax evenly along the length of the skis, so that when they hit sunny or shady spots, their speed would be consistant.

Katherine Ann Morrison was born in Vancouver, BC on February 28th, 1921. Her family then moved up to a cabin sixty miles north of Whitehorse, North West Territories. Her father was a trapper and he was sometimes gone for weeks at a time. The family grew to include three younger brothers. In the early 40s they moved back to Vancouver, and eventually settled in Nanaimo.

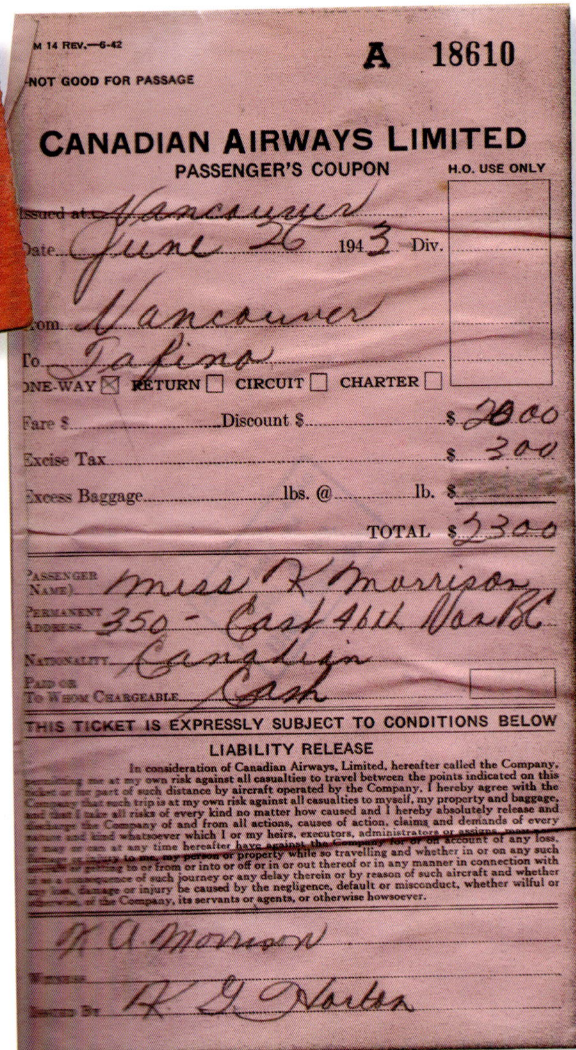

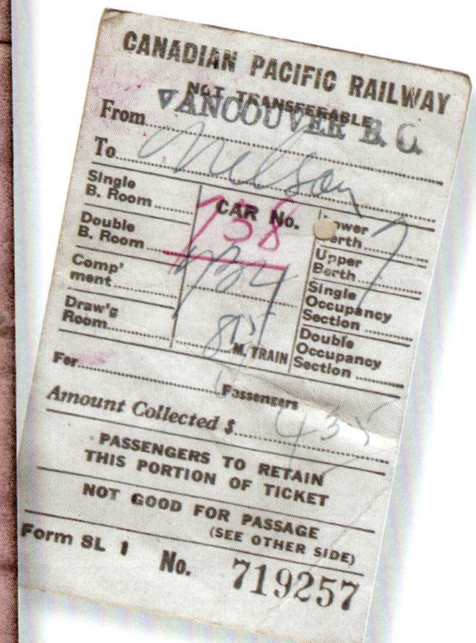

Rene liked to travel between the Mainland and Vancouver Island as well as to other destinations.

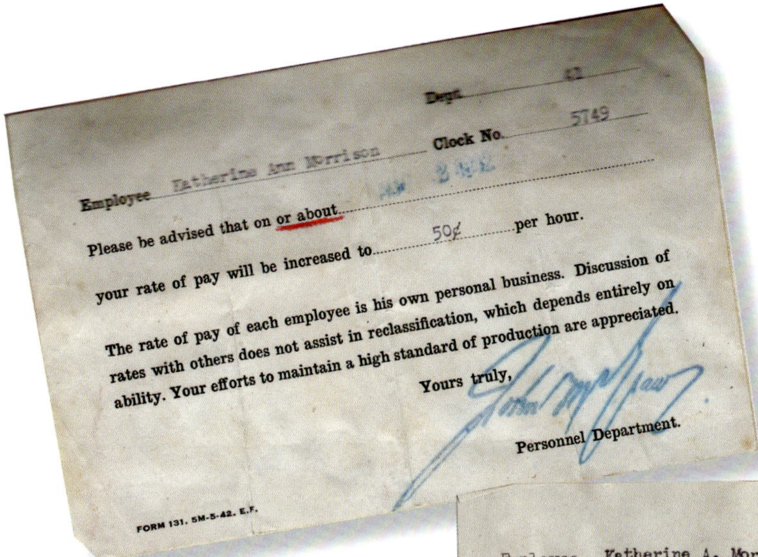

Dept. 41

Employee Katherine Ann Morrison Clock No. 5749

Please be advised that on or about [illegible]

your rate of pay will be increased to 50¢ per hour.

The rate of pay of each employee is his own personal business. Discussion of rates with others does not assist in reclassification, which depends entirely on ability. Your efforts to maintain a high standard of production are appreciated.

Yours truly,

Personnel Department.

FORM 131. 5M-5-42. E.F.

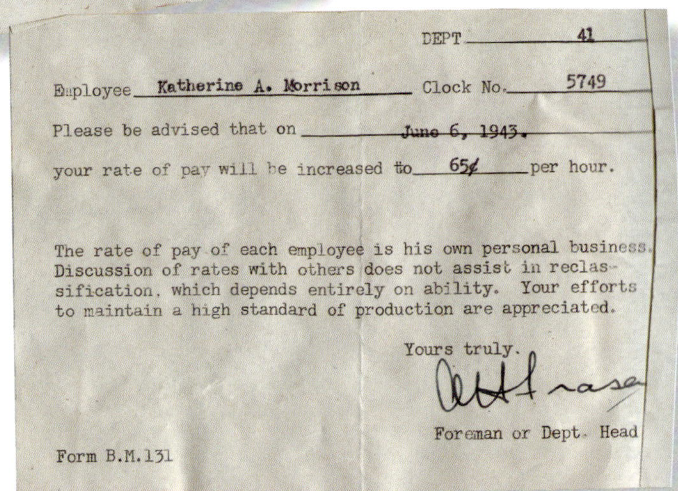

DEPT 41

Employee Katherine A. Morrison Clock No. 5749

Please be advised that on June 6, 1943.

your rate of pay will be increased to 65¢ per hour.

The rate of pay of each employee is his own personal business. Discussion of rates with others does not assist in reclassification, which depends entirely on ability. Your efforts to maintain a high standard of production are appreciated.

Yours truly.

Foreman or Dept. Head

Form B.M.131

In 1942, Rene started working at Boeing for a wage of 50 cents an hour. By 1943 she was making a whopping 65 cents an hour.

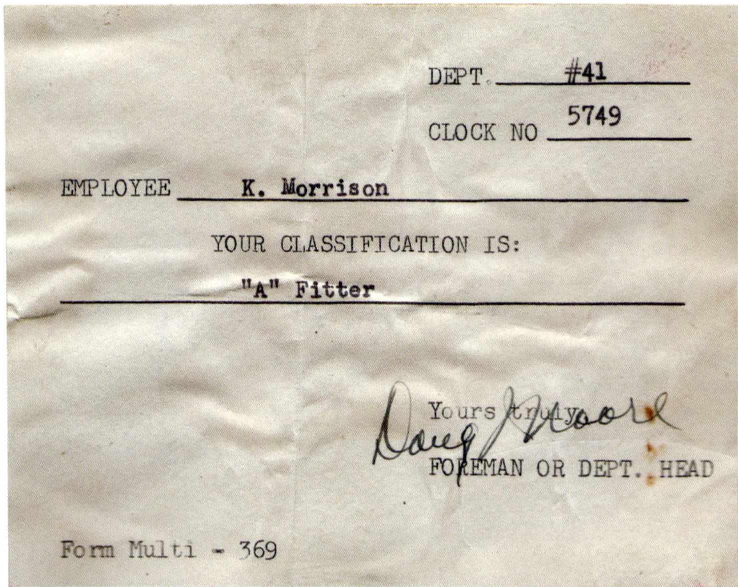

DEPT. #41

CLOCK NO 5749

EMPLOYEE K. Morrison

YOUR CLASSIFICATION IS:

"A" Fitter

Yours truly,

FOREMAN OR DEPT. HEAD

Form Multi - 369

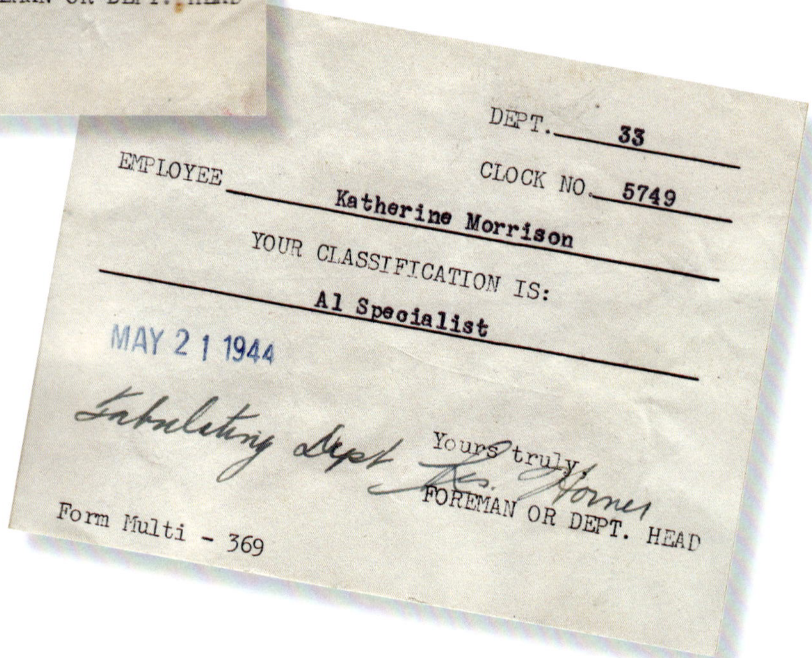

DEPT. 33

CLOCK NO. 5749

EMPLOYEE Katherine Morrison

YOUR CLASSIFICATION IS:

A1 Specialist

MAY 2 1 1944

Fabricating Dept

Yours truly,

FOREMAN OR DEPT. HEAD

Form Multi - 369

Two of the classifications that Rene advanced to during her time at Boeing.

On Sept 29th, 1943, Rene transferred, along with some other Boeing employees, to work in the Nelson. BC plant.

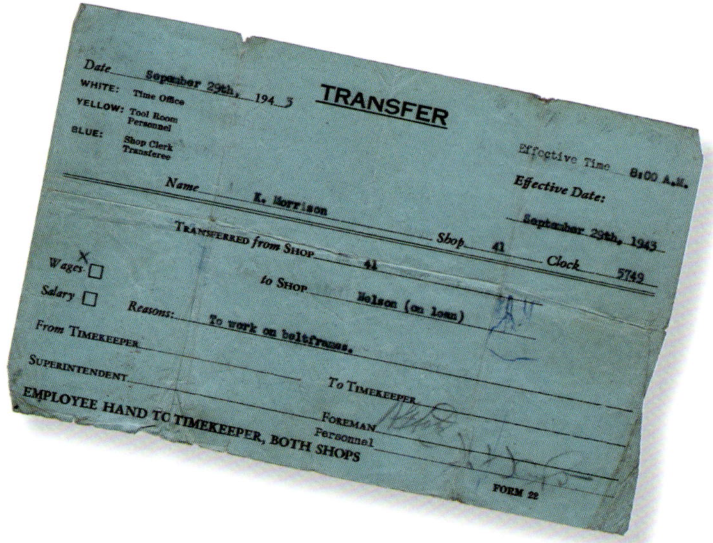
Date September 29th, 1943
WHITE: Time Office
YELLOW: Tool Room Personnel
BLUE: Shop Clerk Transferee

TRANSFER

Effective Time 8:00 A.M.
Effective Date: September 29th, 1943

Name K. Morrison Shop 41
TRANSFERRED from SHOP 41 Clock 5749
Wages ☒ Salary ☐
to SHOP Nelson (on loan)
Reasons: To work on beltframes.
From TIMEKEEPER
SUPERINTENDENT
To TIMEKEEPER
FOREMAN
Personnel
EMPLOYEE HAND TO TIMEKEEPER, BOTH SHOPS
FORM 22

B.S.A. Club and 'Flu Take Over Nelson Plant

We are a little off the **"Beam"** this time. Since the last issue we have elected as **Official Reporter** for Nelson **Miss Elsie Hodgson,** but the 'flu got her this week. We hope she will make her debut next issue.

Amelia Pasternak, last week's correspondent, is also on the sick list which includes our presiding genius **Lois Anderson.** Only hospital case to date is Guard **Al Merz** who is now, we are glad to say, back with us.

The **Social and Athletic Club** now has a membership creeping past the 75 per cent figure. Of course the **Vancouver girls** haven't had to join the club, which reminds us that four more of our girls have returned to the big city . . . **Kay Morrison, Jo Child, Kay Almquist** and **Mary Russell.** We were really sorry to see them go and told them so, at which time all Vancouver girls received a small presentation as a token of our regard.

The **weather** in the shop has been fluctuating within the depressed range of 51 to 55 degrees (Fahrenheit). However what was formerly a rumor appears to have grown up into a fact.

The fact: we are going to have a heating plant.

The proof: some guy is busy chopping holes in the cement wall and pipes are peeping through.

Somewhere along the line, while working at Boeing, Rene got the nickname of Kay, possibly from her co-workers or the young men she knew in the Air Force.

View from Hollyburn.

Harry and Rene out for a stroll on Hollyburn, 1951.

Proud parents with their son, Richard, and the family dog, Christmas, 1953.

Richard having some play time.

Rene and Harry with Richard.

SKIERS IN FOG 1953

Harry Hurries To Win Race

By DON TYRELL 21 SECONDS

Harry Burfield turned his back on the cash customers Sunday on Hollyburn Ridge and went out to win himself a ski race.

Operator of the Hollyburn Ski Camp, and the ski rental concession at Hiview on the Ridge, Harry is usually so busy handling skis he seldom gets to use them. Sunday, however, he took time off, climbed to Hollyburn Peak and groped his way down through the pea-soup fog in 7:29.4 to win his fourth Viski Classic combination downhill and cross country race.

Fog was so thick racers snowplowed slowly down the Shoulder and Romstad's Hill with visibility zero. High up on the peak nearly every racer spilled as they hit the bottom of the steep run.

BURFIELD — On April 5, 1953, Joseph Harry Burfield, aged 73 years, late of 1517 Bellevue Ave., West Vancouver. Survived by his loving wife; 2 sons, Harry and Fred; one grandson, Richard, all of West Vancouver; one sister, Mrs. H. J. Parker, Vancouver. Funeral service Thursday, April 9 at 1:30 p.m. from the Hollyburn Funeral Home, West Vancouver. Mr. R. E. Ferguson officiating. Cremation. No flowers by request.

Harry's father passed away on April 5th, 1953.

Rene and Richard, stretching their legs in Quesnel on a business trip promoting Hollybury Ski Lodge, 1953.

Clipping from
March 30th, 1953.

Courtesy of The
Vancouver Sun

slo Comet' Amazes Crowd
Sun Ski Show on Grouse

ksen Wins Slalom;
n Stages Big Upset

By DON TYRELL

st colorful Viking since Lief Eriksen won new hundreds of new friends for his country on ntain over the weekend.

Stein Eriksen, the "Oslo Comet," whistled off Grouse peak and rocketed down the steep 1200-foot vertical drop, power-diving through 27 sets of control gates at jet plane speed to win The Sun's annual Giant Slalom race.

Announcer Dave Mathews barely had time to say "Here comes Stein" before the Oslo flash and 1952 Olympic Giant Slalom champion was out of sight on the tree-lined course.

BLINDING SPEED

This was the moment the crowd had waited for and the 2000 who lined the snowy trail weren't disappointed. They shook their heads at the blinding speed which dropped Stein from peak to finish line in 1:24.9, nearly 10 seconds ahead of second place John Frazee of Mt. Seymour.

Apart from the spectacular race by Eriksen the honors went mostly to the local hot rods who made runs which would have taken top honors in any field except one paced by a flyer like Stein.

Doug Fraser, last year's winner, finished third while George Merry, of Rossland, a member of Canada's 1952 Olympic team, finished fourth. Roy McConnell and Frank Atkinson placed fifth and sixth. First of the strong American entry to finish was George Mills of the Penguin Ski Club, Seattle.

JEAN SURPRISED

Biggest surprise of the day was the performance turned in by Jean Chalmers in winning the women's race. Jean flashed perfect, natural racing form in a lightning-fast run of 1:40, faster than all but a mere handful of the men racers. She was 12½ seconds ahead of pre-race favorite Sandra Fraser.

It was Jean's second win in the big Sun classic. Her first win came in 1950.

The jumping classes were ruled by the starry local leapers who copped firsts in every bracket. Halvar Sellesback, who injured a knee on Mt. Seymour last week, came back strongly Sunday for a con-

ORTS

SWANGARD
rts Editor

on., Mar. 30

couver
ggers
(B)rink

K RICHARDS
aff Reporter
, Vancouver 2
leads best-of-five
, 2-1)

, March 30.—Van-
uks face elimina-
the Western Hoc-
e playoffs when
Seattle Bombers
fourth game of
five quarter-final
ght.
ically, they are
r it.
ay to Seattle, Sun-
ept talking about
game being "the

★ ★

arently forgot it
g one" for Seattle.
rs were prepared
for it. Canucks

ot been for Emile
the Canucks goal,
would have been
e proved why he
hosen "most valu-
to his team" in

0 fans — the best
wd of the season,
home-town Bomb-
heir rugged fore-
actics right from
faceoff. And Bill
ack in the Bomber

HALVAR SELLESBACK
. . . tops class A jumpers

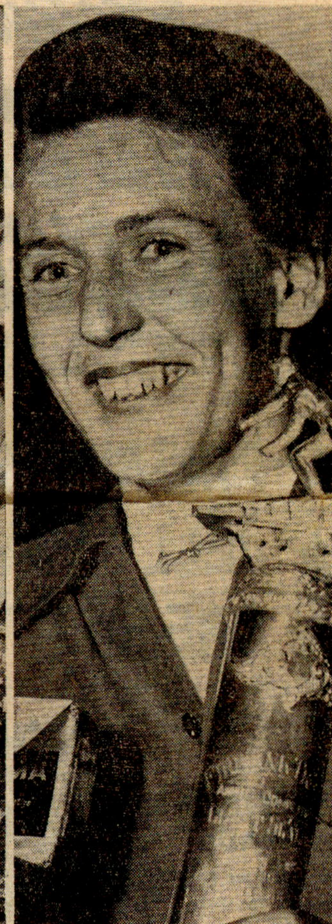

JEAN CHALMERS
. . . slalom champ

Stein Stuns Spectators With Smart Ski Stunts

By DON TYRELL

They're still talking about it around town but even those who saw it can hardly believe it.

Stein Eriksen, the Olympic

Peter wasn't the only one amazed. Chief Sun Ski Instructor Gus Johnson, an outstanding stylist, said: "Seeing a man ski like that makes me want to burn my

fairly shaking Saturday and Sunday to accordion music and rollicking Norwegian songs.

Entries for the city championship ski meet on Grouse

JEAN SURPRISED

Biggest surprise of the day was the performance turned in by Jean Chalmers in winning the women's race. Jean flashed perfect, natural racing form in a lightning-fast run of 1:40, faster than all but a mere handful of the men racers. She was 12½ seconds ahead of pre-race favorite Sandra Fraser.

It was Jean's second win in the big Sun classic. Her first win came in 1950.

The jumping classes were ruled by the starry local leapers who copped firsts in every bracket. Halvar Sellesback, who injured a knee on Mt. Seymour last week, came back strongly Sunday for a convincing win in "A" class. Halvar jumped hard and high in near-perfect form with two [illegible] 134 and 164, the longest jump of the day for 219 points.

HALVAR TOO STRONG

Ted Hunt appeared to be headed for a win after he shaded Halvar's first effort by three feet. Halvar was too strong on his second jump and Ted was pushed back to second place with 206.4 points. Jack Roocroft with 203.9 finished third to give Vancouver Ski Club a clean sweep in the first three jumping spots.

Reidar Ulland of Leavenworth was the best of the American jumpers, finishing fourth with 199.2 points.

Johnny Halstead made two neat jumps to win the "B" class with 200.4 points, two more than Leavenworth's Cliff Montgomery. Ragnar Ulland of Seattle placed third. Mt. Seymour's hustling Harvey Abell was the best of the junior jumpers.

Stein Stuns Spectators With Smart Ski Stunts

By DON TYRELL

They're still talking about it around town but even those who saw it can hardly believe it.

Stein Eriksen, the Olympic Giant Slalom champ and the man who has made swan [illegible] the North American [illegible]ver[illegible]ent, is the man who started all the talk. On Grouse Mountain Saturday and Sunday the smiling Norwegian hurtled down the big hill, dropped his poles and giving a tremendous spring, took off from a small snow jump like a frightened rocket.

At the height of his flight he was in a perfect swan dive, going from there into a quick forward somersault that would do credit to an Olympic diver. He landed perfectly and did three quick turns that had the experts gasping.

★ ★ ★

Peter Vadja, former UBC ski coach and Swiss Universities' ski star, said: "If I hadn't seen I wouldn't believe it and now I've seen it I still can't figure how anybody can have such perfect body control.

Peter wasn't the only one amazed. Chief Sun Ski Instructor Gus Johnson, an outstanding stylist, said: "Seeing a man ski like that makes me want to burn my own boards."

★ ★ ★

[illegible] Norweg[illegible] on Grouse Sunday than in Norway. **Chris Johnson,** 78, and still skiing, was up to wonder at **Stein** and admire the improved form of local jumpers. **Chris Engh,** another old-time Hollyburn jumper, was up.... **Harry Burfield,** of Hollyburn Ski Camp, dusted off his jumpers to place second to **Tom Mobraaten** in the senior jumping....

Somersaults and trick tumbling stunts became popular Sunday afternoon after **Stein** had made his second exhibition. . . . **Gordy Cowan, John Frazee** were flipping off the chalet roof into the deep snow, while **Rolf Helle,** who broke a ski and missed the jumping, kept in shape by doing back flips off the chalet roof. . . .

All in all, it was a wonderful weekend, both indoors and out, the old chalet log walls fairly shaking Saturday and Sunday to accordion music and rollicking Norwegian songs.

Entries for the city championship ski meet on Grouse Mountain close Tuesday. Forms should be sent to [illegible]ing, 500 Beatty Street.

Schedule for the tournament calls for cross-country racing and slalom Friday with cross-country in the morning and slalom in the afternoon. Downhill racing goes Saturday with giant slalom Sunday morning and jumping Sunday afternoon.

Dauphin Wins Title

BRANDON, March 30—(CP)—Dauphin Kings, defending Western Canada intermediate hockey champions, scored an 11-9 win over Lloydminster Huskies here Saturday night after two overtime periods in the fifth and deciding game of their Manitoba-Saskatchewan intermediate series. A sellout crowd of 5000 took in the contest.

Richard standing beside his first pair of skis and his puppy, "Prince", 1954.

One year later. . . Richard had grown a little and Prince had grown a lot.

Harry, Rene and Richard. Another great day on the mountain showing Richard all there was to know about skiing.

Rene and Harry with Richard, winter of '53, Hollyburn.

Skiing was still a big part of Harry's life in the 50s even though he was no longer competing at his previous level.

Harry (left photo) and Fred (right photo) with Roy Raymer. Harry and Fred both volunteered at the outdoor canteen for the competitors at the bottom of Romstead on Hollyburn. They would sell coffee, tea, and hot food to the racers. Harry and Fred were known for their white caps. Fred still wears one to this day.

Harry was always proud that he held the record for the fastest time down Romstead until one day he took a bad fall and Bill Irwin beat him. Harry still finished second that day. On another race Bill Irwin had had a very nasty fall and dislocated his shoulder. He popped it back in place and still managed to come in first.

Harry leaning against the panel truck on the right, holding his well sighted rifle, while hunting at the Chezicut Lake Resort in the Chilcotin, October, 1954.

Cabin B on Hollyburn Mountain, June 1, 1955.

Rene holding Marion at 12 days old with Richard and Prince, June 14, 1955.

Harry with the children, September 1955.

Burfield Tops Hollyburn Ski Runners

Harry Burfield and Ole Johannsen copped the honors in the Hollyburn Ridgers Club championship cross - country races Sunday. Harry had the fastest time of the day to lead the H. P. S. C. members, and Ole, only 10 seconds slower, was head man for the Viskies.

Jack Wood topped the "B" men for the H. P. S. C., his time being 10 seconds behind Max Kranier, the V. S. C. top-notcher.

Ted Yard added a win in the cross-country to his jumping victory in the "C" class for the H. P. S. C., thus taking the combined for his club. Bob Caverley paced the Vancouver Ski Clubbers.

In the junior event Paddy Wing led Jack Roocroft for the Hollyburners. Allan Teasdale, also a victor in last week's jumping, won the Viskie cross-country and the combined of his club.

Ernie Griffiths came home first in the Tyee cross-country event ahead of Ernie Marwick to take "A" class honors.

Bill Wicks played head man for the "B" class racers.

Young Bill Tomlinson headed the Tyee juniors.

Ridgers taking part in next Sunday's downhill and slalom must have their entrees at the Two Skiers by Thursday night. Detailed results:

H. P. S. C.

"A" Class — 1, Harry Burfield, 49:27; 2, Jack Foster, 1:02:52.

"B" Class—1, Jack Woods, 53:41; 2, Bruce Switzer, 1:06:29.

"C" Class—1, Ted Yard, 30:15.

Junior—1, Paddy Wing, 28:19; 2, Jack Roocroft, 29:15.

V. S. C.

"A" Class—1, Ole Johannsen, 49:37; 2, Marius Swedhal, 51:11.

"B" Class—1, Max Kranier, 53:31; 2, J. Owen, 1:02.

"C" Class—1, Bob Caverley, 31:58.

Junior—1, A. Teasdale, 29:08; 2, Don Manning, 31:38; 3, George Sayce, 32:35.

STEVENS.

Skiing

Jumps to Sotvedt

Henry Sotvedt, veteran Vancouver Ski Club jumper, won the Class A jumping contest up at Grouse Mt. yesterday with an average jump of 210 feet. Second place went to Harry Burfield, Hollyburn star.

Roy Farrell, Revelstoke flash, copped honors in the B division.

CLASS "A"

1—Henry Sotvedt, VSC	210.1
2—Harry Burfield, HPSC	199.9
3—Ole Johannsen, VSC	186.5
4—J. Everall, TSC	184
5—Bill Hansen, HPSC	172.3
6—Emil Gunnersen, RCAF	169.6
7—Bill Irwin, 1st Batt., Irish Fusiliers	149.8
8—Art Johnson, VSC	144.2
9—Bud Stevens, TSC	65.9

CLASS "B"

1—Roy Farrell, RSC	205.1
2—Ernie Griffiths, TSC	204.1
3—E. Sandland, Copper Mt.	183.8
4—Max Kramer, VSC	176
5—E. Myra, Copper Mt.	175.6
6—D. Marwick, TSC	171
7—C. Griffiths, Army	143.9
8—George Nash, HPSC	137.5
9—K. Owen, TSC	131.1
10—Dennis, TSC	108.3

Richard with Marion in the Jolly Jumper in the snow, winter of '55, Hollyburn.

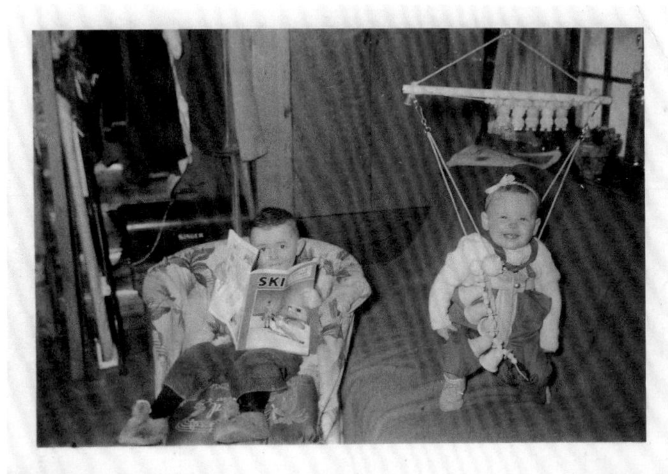

Richard enjoyed reading ski magazines at an early age.

Richard outside Cabin B,
Hollyburn, 1955.

Harry and Marion, winter of '55 and summer of '56.

Like his grandfather, Harry was a great carpenter. Even at work Harry was always smiling. He loved life and embraced every day to it's fullest.

Fred and Evelyn Burfield holding their daughter Peggy, born November 9th, 1956.

source: West Vancouver Archives. Hollyburn Heritage Society Collection. 789.WVA. HHS.BUR

Fred and Evelyn picking berries on Hollyburn and Peggy eating them. Marion remembers doing the same thing when her family went blueberry picking. The mountains always had an abundance of fresh fruit in the summer months.

Bump-Skiing On Hollyburn

HOW TO TAKE THE BUMPS in skiing is here demonstrated by Harry Burfield during a class in the Hollyburn Free Ski School. The three weekly ski classes are held Wednesdays and Saturdays under the sponsorship of the Hollyburn Aerial Trams in

Courtesy of The Vancouver Daily Province

Harry Burfield's
53-foot leap,
May 6, 1956.

source: West
Vancouver Archives.
Hollyburn Heritage
Society collection.
778.MVA.HHS.BUR

Harry on Hollyburn, shows off the skis he used in jumping competitions.

On the North Shore

Ridge Development Committee Formed

WEST VANCOUVER—Plans for development of Hollyburn Ridge were formulated by Municipal Council and interested parties in Municipal Hall Wednesday night.

Delegations from Hollyburn and Westlake ski lodges, Hollyburn Aerial Trams Ltd., Westlake and Vancouver ski clubs, and Norm Deacon Ski Tows were invited to submit plans for the project.

Councillor C. A. Williams urged that a committee from the delegates be formed immediately.

The reeve suggested the name "Ridge Development Committe" and nominated eight men. They are Harry Burfield, Don Lee, Les May Brang Upham, Roy Sim, Jack Buckeridge, Norm Deacon, and a representative from Vancouver Junior Chamber of Commerce.

Wes May outlined plans for a new ski jump in Westlake area, costs of which were estimated at $10,000.

Roy Sim, president of Hollyburn Aerial Trams Ltd., said his company would be behind any constructive projects outlined by the committee.

"I will go so far as to say we will assist the financing of the proposed ski jump, as it is one of the prime necessities for tourist attraction, as well as local competition," he said.

A further meeting will be held when the forest engineer, Herb Johnson, has a complete report for council.

There was always work to be done in order to live comfortably on the mountain. Harry was always up for the challenge.

Harry taking a break in the sun from his carpentry work on Hollyburn.

There was always time for Prince. He was a wonderful dog and everyone in the family loved him. In the summertime, the children loved to go running into the lake, screaming and hollering. Prince would drag them out and they'd go running back in again. Because of his Newfoundland breeding, Prince's instinct was to rescue the children.

Marion and Prince outside their home in North Vancouver, 1959.

Christmas dinner, 1958.

Richard and Marion reading bedtime stories together.

Poster for the Highview Lodge Turkey Dinner with Richard and Prince on the chairlift.

"In 1950, Hi Coville and his partners built a chairlift up Hollyburn Mountain and started construction of Highview lodge at the top. I remember the lodge took 2 years to build because the building contractor used huge old growth logs from the mountain that were difficult to move into place. In between construction seasons, they had to cover the lodge's roof with building paper to protect it because they did not finish the roof before the snow came. When the lodge was completed my brother Harry moved his ski shop there and skiers got their skies from him then hiked to either Westlake Lodge or Hollyburn Lodge to ski on their rope tows. The lodge had a great view of the city but was very hard to heat. One winter they brought in 700 gallons of oil to heat the building and it was used up in two weeks. Oscar Pearson, who worked at the top of the chairlift, suggested that they start using wood for heat instead of oil. Oscar did the woodcutting for the fireplace and a wood stove heater was installed to heat the lodge. Highview burned down in June of 1965, under suspicious circumstances, not long after the chairlift stopped running and the company went into receivership."

—Fred Burfield

Richard and Marion with their grandmother.

When the family lived in Vancouver, they'd often visit Stanley Park and go out for lunch at the one of the local drive-in's where you flashed your car lights to tell the servers you were ready to order. The food came on a long tray that stretched across the front seat from window to window. Harry would joke with his family that he had to have a taste of the children's food before giving it to them, "just in case it was poison".

Marion, always trying to help out.

Richard (far left in the front row) not looking very happy about school—perhaps he'd rather be skiing? In the summer of '61 the family moved to White Croft Village near Kamloops, BC.

The cabins in summertime on Hollyburn. The diving board on the left got lots of use in July and August on the mountain.

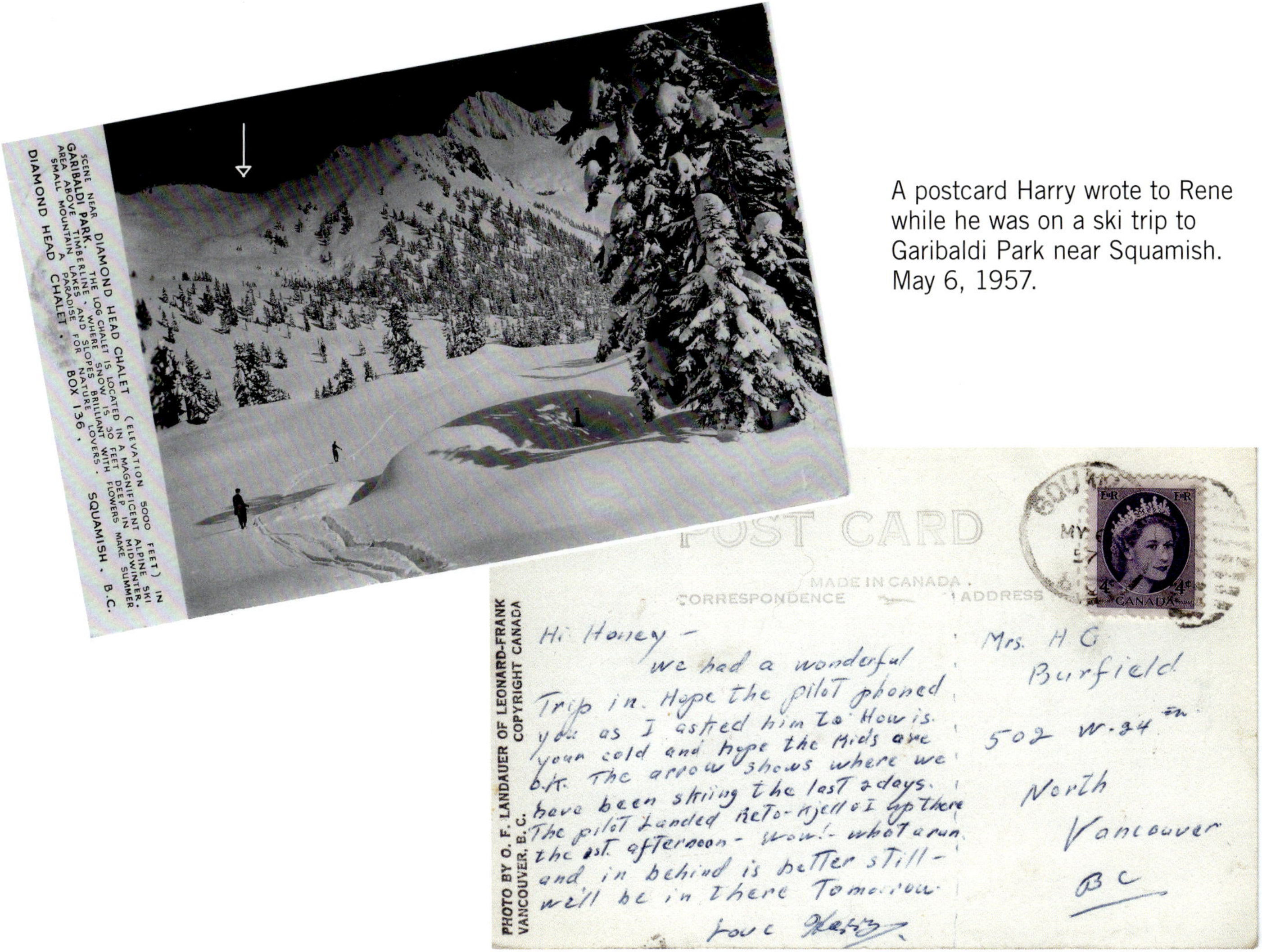

A postcard Harry wrote to Rene while he was on a ski trip to Garibaldi Park near Squamish. May 6, 1957.

Hollyburn Mountain had many ups and downs over the years. With Grouse Mountain and Mount Seymour becoming more accessible and after the fire at the Highview Lodge in 1965, Hollyburn Mountain faded from popularity for more than 20 years. Very few visitors came except for the dedicated cabin owners and their families.

In 1973 the area was designated Cypress Provincial Park and although people still had to hike in to the mountain, a new highway was put in which improved access to Hollyburn.

Fred, Harry and Richard collecting wood on the John Deere tractor.

Fred and Harry working on the John Deere Tractor on Hollyburn Mountain, June 1950s.

source: West Vancouver Archives. Hollyburn Heritage Society Collection
1172D.WVA.HHS.HAR

F. Becker 1961

Chapter Five

Tod Mountain (Sun Peaks)

Harry had come up to Tod Mountain to help build the main lodge. He later returned to the mountain, from Vancouver, with the family in the summer of 1961. He was asked to come back and run the ski shop in the lodge and assist in clearing the land for the many ski runs.

During a lunch break one day, a very curious moose came and startled Harry by putting his front hooves on the tracks of the bulldozer. That was a story he loved to recount with family and friends.

Harry was a very funny man with a wonderful zest for life. His English sense of humour would come out often. He loved to scare Rene by spinning the car around on the icy back roads, but Richard and Marion got a great kick out of it. He always bought station wagons so there would always be plenty of room for ski

facing page: This painting by R. Becker in 1966 was presented to Rene when the lodge at Sun Peaks was named after Harry in 1971.

equipment. On one part of the old road up to Tod Mountain, a steep downgrade followed by a steep upgrade. Harry loved to get airborne when the car got to the top of the hill. Richard and Marion enjoyed the thrill of "losing their tummies" and laughing in the back seat.

After moving to the Kamloops area, the first family home was the house behind the old school on the White Croft Ranch. The homestead was a landmark for many years after the Burfield's moved out, but unfortunately the house was torn down in about 1980.

After the opening of Tod Mountain in the fall of 1961, Harry continued to work for the mountain until the family moved into Kamloops in 1963. At that time Harry and Rene took over *Colly's Tackle Shop*, located at 266 Victoria Street and renamed it *Harry Burfield's Ski and Sport Shop*. In 1964 they moved the store to 145 Victoria Street, where for many years it was a very successful business. The store sold year-round ski, camping, fishing, hiking and hunting supplies and was a friendly and inviting place to visit. Harry's enthusiasm for skiing was shared with anyone who walked through his doors. He wanted everyone to know that skiing was for anybody who wanted to learn.

One of the great things the store offered new little skiers was the ski equipment exchange program. Families could sign up for this program and pay a one-time fee of $20. They would bring their children in at the beginning of the ski season to be fitted with used skis, boots and poles before going off to enjoy the winter fun. The following fall they would return with their

Harry at the store with a customer who came to show off his catch of the day.

gear and exchange it for the next size in used equipment, at no additional cost. If the children did not want to pursue the sport, they just brought the equipment back and it would go to the next generation of little skiers. This successful program continued, year after year, until the children reached 12 years of age.

As a newcomer to the Kamloops area, Harry knew the importance of hiring people to work with him. Staff at the shop included familiar people like Jack Shaw, whose knowledge of fly fishing in the area was a great asset. Jack Shaw went on to write books on fly fishing on BC interior lakes and rivers. Rob White was also a great person to have working in the store. It was also important to have reliable staff working at the store with Harry and Rene travelling to trade shows throughout Canada and the United States to bring back all the latest equipment, clothing and ideas to keep the public excited about all outdoor activities.

Many regular patrons of the store became very successful business people. Like Mike Wiegele who operates a world class Helicopter Skiing and Heli Snowboarding resort in Blue River.

Harry was a man of many talents—a wonderful family man, a terrific ski jumper and a highly competent businessman. In addition to the store in Kamloops, he and Rene opened a ski shop in what's known today as the Burfield Lodge at Sun Peaks, where they rented out ski equipment for the day or the week.

In addition to all of his other endeavors, Harry also had a fifteen minute outdoor television program called *Sports View* on the local Kamloops channel CFJC. Every Friday evening, after the local news, Harry would interview sports minded people who were involved in all kinds of outdoor activities. On June 11, 1971 Harry hosted his last show.

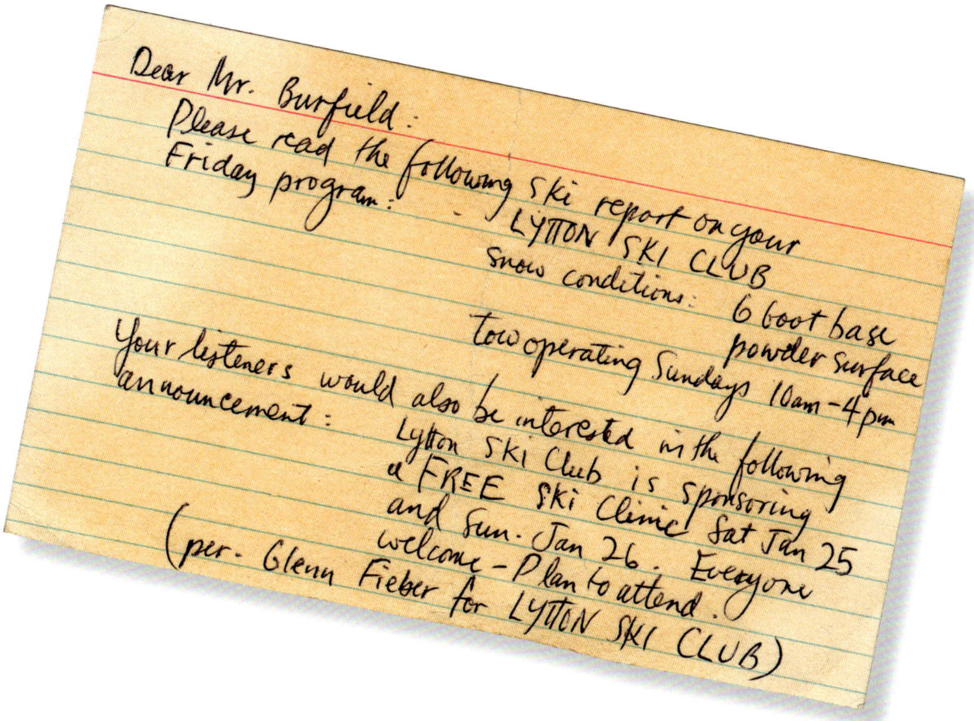

Dear Mr. Burfield:
Please read the following ski report on your Friday program: - LYTTON SKI CLUB
Snow conditions: 6 foot base
powder surface
tow operating Sundays 10am-4pm
Your listeners would also be interested in the following announcement: Lytton Ski Club is sponsoring a FREE Ski Clinic Sat Jan 25 and Sun. Jan 26. Everyone welcome - Plan to attend.
(per. Glenn Fieber for LYTTON SKI CLUB)

Dear Marion,

What a surprise to hear from you. Your request [for details about working with our mom and dad] certainly triggered a lot of memories. I first met your Dad on the ridge run when I was coming down the mountain from putting the cattle up. They had just bulldozed the ridge run and your Dad was clearing stumps with Ralph Nelson. I would guess it would have been the summer of 1961. I remember your Dad had the ski shop in the day lodge. I rented a pair of boots and skis for my first venture on the mountain as a skier. I fell near tower 22 and sprained my ankle which resulted in my first tobbagan ride with Ueli Steiner on the handle bars. I got back on skis after McKonkey took over the shop from your Dad. I remember that was a bit of a messy period.

I started to drive the school bus in 1969 and worked part time for your Dad when I had to take the bus into town for servicing. My first job was changing springs in Tyrolia bindings. From there I graduated upstairs to selling skis and mounting bindings. By 1968 McKonkeys had left and that was the year the lift burned. I set up a small shop outside the lodge for your Dad in a small shack the mountain pulled in for the shop. I ran this shop a few days a week but there wasn't much business. In the meantime your Dad had started the small shop at Grandview, which I worked in on the days the school kids came for lessons.

My brother-in-law Jack Brady and I were working in our workshop on June 12, 1971 when we heard an airplane motor and looked up to see the float plane crossing the valley toward Tod. It was a really stormy day, with low cloud and rain. The next day we heard the tragic news. From then on I worked in the shop in town five days a week from 9 until 3 except on days I had to take field trips with the bus. After the ski season I started to work with Jack Shaw in the fly-tying section, putting material in little bags and learning all about that part of the business. I would take the summer months off to work at home. This routine went on for 72/73 seasons. It was at this time I think that the shop was having some difficulties. Your Mom tried to talk me into managing the shop but I was in the middle of selling our ranch and did not want any more responsibilities. Dave Rowe and Mike Manchee were still there but obviously couldn't come to an agreement with your Mom. By November1973 your Mom was talking of selling the shop, her personal problems were starting to over whelm her. My last day at the shop was March 27, 1975.

One of the more amusing stories I remember was with Ruth McKeene when she worked at the store. At that time I had a student on the bus that would bring me an off-color joke every afternoon which I would repeat the next morning in the shop. Ruth would act scandalized at hearing the story but couldn't resist listening. Everyone seemed to enjoy the joke and it lightened the atmosphere in the shop.

Mike Manchee was the ski boot expert when the foam boots made their appearance and it seemed all the odd-shaped feet in town turned up for a fitting.

When Jim McKonkey was teaching a class on Tod, one day in the Crystal bowl, he was trying to get his class to ski the new feet together method. After expounding at great length about the merits of the new technique he looked up and here comes Harry Burfield on his Telemark skis doing the exact opposite of what he had been teaching. Long graceful turns with one foot off the snow in perfect balance, then another turn in the other direction. Jim commented, "That is a perfect turn, but don't do it that way. Oh heck lets just ski!"

All the kids that worked at the shop really fit in well and were treated exceptionally well by your Mom. Jack Shaw was a prince of a man and had a wealth of fishing knowledge. I think Jack could catch fish where there were none. I went to Jocko lake with him at noon hour once and he caught 2 in 15 minutes. I was sorry I did not spend more time with him but I did get to know his wife in later years when I was researching the history of our valley.

Your Mom and Dad are dear to me. They were both fair and honest in all things.

All the best,
Rob White

Marion on Tod Mountain, 1963. Some days in the winter, the weather was so bad they would cover us with capes for the ride up the chair. The attendants at the top would bundle the capes up and send them back down on the empty seats.

The Burfield's mobile home in 1962. It was located where the entrance currently is to the White Croft Village.

Marion at the age of 6, outside the Burfield Lodge.

There was plenty to do during the summers months on Tod Mountain. Millions of flowers bloom in August up in the Alpine Meadows.

During a trail ride on the back side of Tod Mountain. (from left) Marion Burfield, George Winters (owner of the horses), Rene and Richard Burfield, 1962.

Half way up the old Burfiield chair lift, summer of 1962. Summers were beautiful on the mountain.

SUNRISE, SUNSET TIMES, KAMLOOPS
Sunday, March 15
Sun rises .... 6:18 a.m.
Sun sets .... 6:06 p.m.
(Standard Time)

KAMLOO

The Ho

EIGHTY-FIFTH YEAR— No. 63

KAMLO

MINISTER OPENS CHAMPIONSHIPS

Northern Affairs Minister Arthur Laing chats with three officials Friday after he had opened the Canadian senior alpine ski championships on Mount Tod. Officials, left to right, are: Bob Bartley, chief starter; Arnold Midgely, chief referee for the Canadian Amateur Ski Association, and Harry Burfield, chief of the course.

—Sentinel Photo

Marion and Prince in the front yard on Nicola Street, Kamloops. This picture was taken by a local photographer and sent to the local newspaper, 1964.

Rene and Harry flew to Montreal for Expo '67 as well as a ski trade show. For the return trip they purchased this station wagon and drove back across Canada to Kamloops. This photograph of the family was taken outside their home on Townsend Place, Brocklehurst.

Marion and Rick, October 1967.

Harry and Rene both loved fishing. It was one of the many passions they shared.

Tyrolia
12

Chapter 6

Tragedy Strikes

On Saturday, June 12, 1971, Harry left the store and drove out to the Kamloops airport to meet a young couple, Wolfgang Ehmann, a ski acrobatics champion, and Christine Sauders, both from Calgary, Alberta. He took them back to meet Rene and see the store before driving out to Westsyde, where Harry and his family lived. Rene stayed to close down the store for the day. Later that day, Harry chartered Harold Palmer and his float plane to take them on a sight-seeing tour because Harry and the young couple were interested in purchasing Tod Mountain.

Marion remembers waving good-bye to them from their balcony as the float plane taxied up the North Thompson River and took off for what was supposed to be a 60-minute tour. Tragically, they never returned. The plane went down in

facing page: This photograph of Harry is believed to show his last race on April 3, 1971, at Apex Mountain, Pentiction. (see stats on next page).

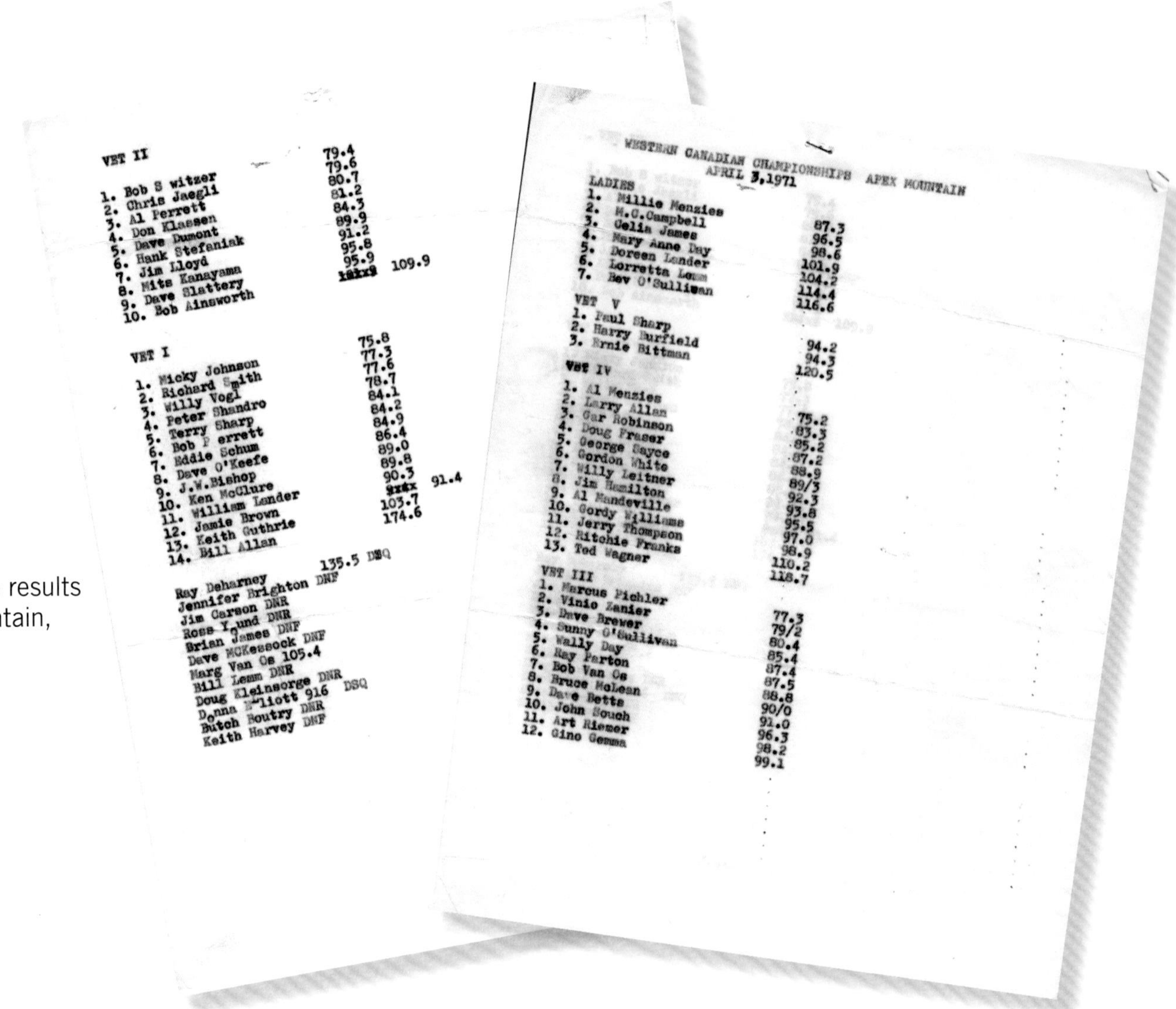

VET II

1. Bob S witzer 79.4
2. Chris Jaegli 79.6
3. Al Perrett 80.7
4. Don Klassen 81.2
5. Dave Dumont 84.3
6. Hank Stefaniak 89.9
7. Jim Lloyd 91.2
8. Mits Kanayama 95.8
9. Dave Slattery 95.9
10. Bob Ainsworth ~~[illegible]~~ 109.9

VET I

1. Micky Johnson 75.8
2. Richard Smith 77.3
3. Willy Vogl 77.6
4. Peter Shandro 78.7
5. Terry Sharp 84.1
6. Bob P errett 84.2
7. Eddie Schum 84.9
8. Dave O'Keefe 86.4
9. J.W.Bishop 89.0
10. Ken McClure 89.8
11. William Lander 90.3
12. Jamie Brown ~~[illegible]~~ 91.4
13. Keith Guthrie 103.7
14. Bill Allan 174.6

Ray Deharney 135.5 DSQ
Jennifer Brighton DNF
Jim Carson DNR
Ross Y und DNR
Brian James DNF
Dave McKessock DNF
Marg Van Os 105.4
Bill Lemm DNR
Doug Kleinsorge DNR
Donna Elliott 916 DSQ
Butch Boutry DNR
Keith Harvey DNF

WESTERN CANADIAN CHAMPIONSHIPS APEX MOUNTAIN
APRIL 3,1971

LADIES

1. Millie Menzies 87.3
2. M.C.Campbell 96.5
3. Celia James 98.6
4. Mary Anne Day 101.9
5. Doreen Lander 104.2
6. Lorretta Lemm 114.4
7. Bev O'Sullivan 116.6

VET V

1. Paul Sharp 94.2
2. Harry Burfield 94.3
3. Ernie Bittman 120.5

VET IV

1. Al Menzies 75.2
2. Larry Allan 83.3
3. Gar Robinson 85.2
4. Doug Fraser 87.2
5. George Sayce 88.9
6. Gordon White 89/3
7. Willy Leitner 92.3
8. Jim Hamilton 93.8
9. Al Mandeville 95.5
10. Gordy Williams 97.0
11. Jerry Thompson 98.9
12. Ritchie Franks 110.2
13. Ted Wagner 118.7

VET III

1. Marcus Pichler 77.3
2. Vinio Zanier 79/2
3. Dave Brewer 80.4
4. Sunny O'Sullivan 85.4
5. Wally Day 87.4
6. Ray Parton 87.5
7. Bob Van Os 88.8
8. Bruce McLean 90/0
9. Dave Betts 91.0
10. John Souch 96.3
11. Art Riemer 98.2
12. Gino Gemma 99.1

Harry's last race results from Apex Mountain, 1971.

the Seven Mile Meadows on the back side of Tod Mountain. All four perished. It was later determined that the crash was caused by a wind inversion, which occurs when the wind comes over the mountains and pushes down. They had no chance of flying out of the inversion from such a narrow valley.

After Harry's untimely death, in honour of his love of skiing and his efforts to help establish Tod Mountain as a world class ski resort, the owners of the mountain named a chair lift and the lodge after him. Later Burfield Drive and Burfield Heights were also named in his honour as well as Harry's Run at the top of the Burfield Chair.

S DAILY SENTINEL
1871-1971
Newspaper for South Central British Columbia
S, BRITISH COLUMBIA, MONDAY, JUNE 14, 1971 26 Pages NOT OVER TEN CENTS

Tod Mt. air crash takes lives of four

FLOAT PLANE LEAVES KAMLOOPS
. . . to join search for missing aircraft

Two Kamloops men killed

Four persons, including two Kamloops businessmen and the Canadian Ski Acrobatics champion, were killed Saturday when a Cessna 180 float plane crashed into the north side of Tod Mountain, 25 miles northeast of Kamloops.

Dead are Harold Palmer, about 30, of Westsyde, pilot of the aircraft and president of R. and H. Cement Products; Harry Burfield, about 50, owner of Burfield's Ski and Sport Shop; ski champion Wolfgang Ehman, 23, of Calgary; and Christine Saunders, 21, of Calgary.

On sightseeing trip

The aircraft crashed into the north side of the ski mountain at about the 6,000-foot level while on a 60 minute sightseeing trip Saturday afternoon.

It failed to return after taking off at 4 p.m. and a search was started in the Tod Mountain area Sunday.

A Canadian Armed Forces Buffalo aircraft and a Labroador Helicopter from 442 Search and Rescue Squadron at Comox joined in the search.

The helicopter discovered the crash site about 20 minutes after it left Kamloops. All four bodies were airlifted to Kamloops airport aboard the helicopter and were removed to Schoening's Funeral Chapel.

Funeral arrangements for the four had not been confirmed this morning.

In addition to operating a major sporting goods store in Kamloops, Mr. Burfield was considered one of the pioneers of skiing in British Columbia.

He hosted a weekly outdoor program on television which featured information about skiing, hunting and fishing.

He was associated with the development of Grouse Mountain, Vancouver, as a skiing area, and competed in ski-jumping competitions at the Kamloops Ski Hill and other B.C. locations agains well-known skiers like Nels Neslon, after whom the Revelstoke ski jumping hill is named.

Department of Transport investigators, as well as investigators from the Attorney-General's department, were to arrive in Kamloops today to begin an inquiry into the fatal crash.

Forty-first year No. 66 Kamloops, B.C. Monday, June 14, 1971 8 Pages Published Monday-Wednesday-Friday

SEARCH FINDS WRECKAGE

Four killed in Tod Mtn. air crash

Staff Photo by Neil MacDonald

AIR RESCUE helicopter sets down at district RCMP headquarters after search for missing plane. Wreckage was found above 6,000 ft. level of Tod Mtn.

Four people were killed Saturday when their Cessna 180 aircraft crashed into the north slope of Tod Mountain. The wreckage was discovered yesterday and the bodies were brought out by helicopter.

The dead were identified this morning by district RCMP as Harold Palmer of Westsyde, in his 30's or 40's, owner and pilot of the plane; Harry Burfield of Kamloops, in his 50's; Wolfgang Ehman of Calgary, 23; and Christine Saunders, about 21, also of Calgary.

The aircraft disappeared Saturday after it took off for what was believed to be a one-hour site-seeing tour of the Tod Mountain area. The wreckage of the float-equipped aircraft was found above the 6,000 ft. level of Tod Mountain, about 25 miles northeast of Kamloops.

When the plane had still not returned by about 6 p.m. Saturday, two hours after it took off, preparations were begun for a search.

A twin-engine Hercules helicopter was brought in from Search and Rescue in Comox and some local support was given but bad weather prevented much participation by local aircraft.

The search continued underway Sunday.

At about 3 p.m. the search was called off and at 3:15 the helicopter landed at district RCMP headquarters and took on a passenger or passengers, then took off again at 4 p.m., returning at about 5:20 p.m. A short time later RCMP announced that the plane had been found and all aboard were dead.

Mr. Palmer's name was released earlier but the names of his three passengers were withheld until this morn ng pending notification of next of kin.

Mr. Palmer, of Westsyde, was president of R&H Cement Products.

Mr. Burfield, owner of a ski and sport shop in Kamloops, was well - known in the sporting world locally.

The Department of Transport is investigating the cause of the crash.

300 at service for crash victims

More than 300 people attended memorial services yesterday for the four persons killed in the crash of a float plane near Tod Mountain Saturday afternoon.

The dead included Harold Palmer, president of R. and H. Cement Products, 43; Harry Burfield, owner of Burfield's Ski and Sport Shop, 55, both of Westsyde; Wolfgang Ehmann, Canadian Ski Acrobatics Champion, 23, of Calgary; and Christine Saunders, 24, of Exeter, England.

Rev. Victor Kerr conducted the memorial service at St. Paul's Cathedral. It lasted just 30 minutes.

Among the mourners were businessmen, sportsmen, conservationists, skiers and pilots.

Rev. Kerr said that the fullness of life is not always measured in the length of a life.

"Harold, Harry, Wolfgang and Christine all enjoyed a fullness of life because they spent much of their time flying or skiing," he said.

"They experienced a fullness for life because they were able to spend much of their times in the out of doors, away from the concrete jungle."

The remains of Mr. Palmer and Mr. Burfield were cremated following the service, while the bodies of Mr. Ehmann and Miss Saunders were forwarded to their homes in Calgary and England.

Air crash inquest adjourned

A coroner's inquest jury was sworn in last night to investigate Saturday's fatal air crash on Tod Mountain which claimed the lives of four people, including two city businessmen and a national ski champion.

The inquest was adjourned until July 14 pending completion of a Department of Transport inquiry into the crash, which occured at the 6,000-foot level on the north side of the ski mountain.

Killed in the crash were pilot, Harold Palmer, president of R and H Cement, Harry Burfield, owne. of Burfield Ski and Sport Shop, both of Westsyde; Canadian Ski Acrobatics champion Wolfgang Ehmann and Christine Saunders, both of Calgary.

THE LOCAL OUTDOOR scene has suffered a blow by the tragic death, in last weekend's plane crash, of Harry Burfield. He was a member of the Kamloops Fish and Game Association, and had given quite a bit of active time to its activities, despite the calls of successfully running a growing business. He will be sadly missed from the ranks of local business. He will be sadly missed from the ranks of local fishermen and hunters, as he will also be by the sport of skiing in which he was a skilled exponent of long experience.

12A Kamloops Daily Sentinel, Fri., Mar. 10, 1972

[redacted]

Skiing is believing

By NEIL WILLIAMS
Scene Ski Writer

Last week I mentioned that two chairlifts at Tod Mt. could be open that weekend. That still stands.

The new chair might be ready and the other chair might be fixed in time for this weekends skiing and ski race, **The Harry Burfield Memorial**.

Parts had been sent to England, of all places, for replacement when the chair broke down last month some time, and were promptly returned and just as promptly lost en route. A new set was sent over to be matched up for replacement, and is expected to be on the mountain and fitted into the lift before the weekend.

Meanwhile, back to the construction site for the new lift, electricians are working out all the little things to complete the lift. The chair has been running but there are still a number of those small details which have to be worked out before people can get on the chairs.

The chairs, by the way, were supposed to be hung last night, if all goes well, in preparation for a visit by the Department of Transport examiner on Friday. He was scheduled for last Friday, but the extra week was needed to make sure everything was correct.

LONGER SEASON

The lift will provide some great skiing on a north slope, which should allow Tod to remain open for a longer season this spring. It might also give them a chance to recoup some of the losses suffered by the breakdowns.

When a lift breaks down, there must be a reason, and when it breaks down on a regular basis, there must be a very interesting reason. In this case it might be easy to sluff the blame onto last year's management for their disinterest in maintainence, but that is probably as good a reason for the breakdowns as any.

But things are bound to improve under present management, so a wait-and-see attitude will have to be adopted.

March is a busy month for Tod Mt., when they open, with the race to be held this weekend and **Super Sunday** to be staged March 26.

Super Sunday will be one of those days when skiers can do what they normally do, but everyone thinks its kind of dumb, but fun. There will be costumes, and prizes for the best, and novelty races including inner tube races, obstacle races and boat? races.

The **Rube Band** will be there, and might even play some music. More music will be played the night before, at the Saturday night dance in the lodge.

The race that is to be held this weekend will be a double giant slalom race, with B and C class competitors going for the Harry Burfield Memorial Trophy.

Harry was a well-known skier and ski promoter until his tragic death last summer on Tod Mt.

The trophy will honor Harry by its presentation at the major race at Tod Mt. each year, whether it be a B and C class race or an International A class race.

'A' CLASS RACER

Harry was an A class racer himself, and had represented Canada in International skiing. He came to Kamloops in 1961, from Vancouver where he owned Hollyburn ski resort, to help develop Tod Mt. He didn't open the **Harry Burfield Ski and Sport** shop until 1964.

According to "Who's Who in British Columbia," Harry was "a charter member of Intersport Canada . . . and has skied competitively since the age of 15, and had represented Canada in international competition."

The two GS races will be held

The two GS races will be held on the Expo run, and to date, 94 entries have been received.

B class racers will be coming from all over B.C. and the Yukon, and C class racers will come from the Okanagan, Kamloops and Prince George areas.

It is shaping up to be an interesting race, but in their now familiar tradition, the **Kamloops Ski Team** will run away with all the top spots.

Speaking of the ski team, they have been receiving a great deal on support in Kamloops by various groups and people.

One in particular I would like to comment on is **Darryl Henry** at the West Kamloops Home station who has been putting the gas in all the cars that are taking the team to out of town races.

The **Tod Mt. Ski Club**, sponsors of the team, and all skiers, appreciate this kind of service.

Marion:

Bill, Just wrote a letter to all suggesting that you all come here for Christmas, as I have no transportation nor iniciative to leave Rossland I gave him a phone number and a map to my place. If you want to leave a messa-ge on your plans, phone 362-5544 its Scotts number. Bring along your skiis as there is some of the best skiing in Canada here and Its snowing to beat hell, weve been skiing for 2 weeks already Do you rember Tom Irwan well he's here with the National Team, who are here training

I sure hope Ive got your box number right as I lost your letter somewhere. It promises to be a good Christmas around here, lots of parties, food booze ect.

Hope to hear from you soon.

Rick

The last letter Marion received from Rick, 1974.

Richard loved the mountains as much as his father did. If he could have skied all year round, he would have. Richard worked at various ski hills just so that he could spend as much as possible in the mountains. He worked at Tod Mountian (Sun Peaks) before leaving for Invermere in 1972. One of his favourite jobs was working to prepare ski race courses at Panorama Ski Resort. Richard loved the Kootenay, BC area resorts. Red Mountain in Rossland, White Water, outside Nelson, and Apex Mountain in Penticton, were some of his favorites.

On March 21, 1977, tragedy struck the Burfield family once again when Richard was killed in an avalanche on a mountain in the central interior of BC. He had just taken a tumble and was putting his skis back on when the snow buried him. His friend, who was standing right beside him when the avalanche hit, was able to ski almost clear of it. The wall of snow hit him too, but he was fortunate to survive with minor injuries. Richard was not so lucky. By the time his

Rick was always ready for skiing with his lace-up boots around his neck.

friends were able to find him and dig through the 9 feet of snow he was burried under, he had suffocated.

"Avalanche claims local skier" read the Kamloops newspapers on March 22, 1977. "Richard Joseph Burfeld, at the young age of 27, died Monday, March 21, 1977, burried under a 9 foot deep, 3000 cubic food snowslide, on a central interior BC mountian. Rick was one of two skiers that were caught by the avalanche. His ski companion was able to dig himself out but still had to be hospitalized for exposure, hypothermia and shock. Two other skiers who were with the group escaped the slide and were able to find Rick within 20 minutes but he had passed away from asphyxiation. His death was ruled an accident." Within a 2 month period that year, avalanches claimed six other lives in BC and Alberta. It's the chance skiers take when they leave the groomed runs for the back country.

Hot Dogging was Rick's favourite pastime on the mountians.

Rene's business card after she became sole owner of the store.

Rene was overwhelmed with grief after the loss of Harry and then the loss of her only son, Richard. She managed to keep the ski and sports shop in Kamloops open until 1981 when it became too much for her to hang on to the family's dreams. Rene moved out of the Kamloops area and opened her own store in Sorrento, BC. She kept this store open for a few years before finally settling in the Salmon Arm area where her battle with dementia and the hardships of her life took her away on June 17, 2006.

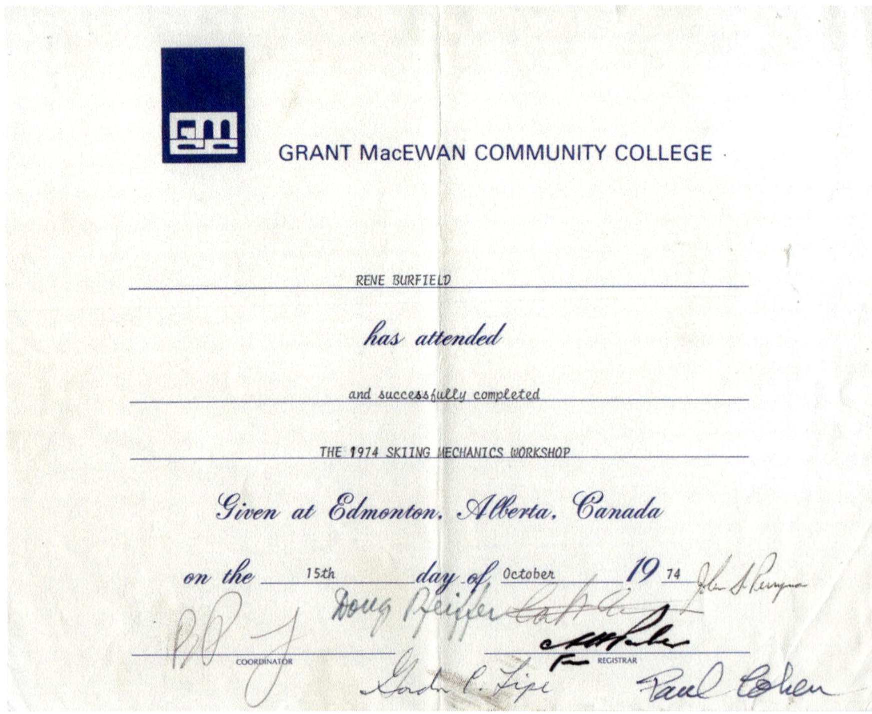
GRANT MacEWAN COMMUNITY COLLEGE

RENE BURFIELD

has attended

and successfully completed

THE 1974 SKIING MECHANICS WORKSHOP

Given at Edmonton, Alberta, Canada

on the 15th *day of* October *19* 74

COORDINATOR REGISTRAR

Harry Burfield

In 1991 the family held a 20-year memorial for Harry at the Burfield Lodge. A large collection of Harry's freshly polished trophies were on display and a special viewing of Harry's last television show featured Harry's interview with Jack Shaw about fishing and tying flies.

Fred Burfield, seated in front of the restored John Deere tractor, with daughter Peggy Burfield (left) and grandchildren Shawna (behind) and Trevor (right), Hollyburn, June 2011.

Wednesday, June 29, 2011 - **North Shore News - A3**

Restored tractor returns to Hollyburn

John Deere 'crawler' left to rust for 25 years

Loren Romei

lromei@nsnews.com

AFTER years of waiting, the Burfield family's John Deere tractor has been restored to its former glory and is ready to be put on display to celebrate Hollyburn Mountain's history.

NEWS photo Cindy Goodman

HOLLYBURN Lodge old-timers Bob Tapp (from left), Gordon Knight, Alex Swanson, Bert Baker and Fred Burfield surround the refurbished John Deere "crawler" that was used to clear pathways around the cabins and routes to Hollyburn Lodge near Cypress Mountain. The tractor was last used in the spring of 1985, but with the work of volunteers and the generosity of John Deere the machine is gloriously restored.

Bob Tapp, the co-chair of the Hollyburn Heritage Society, and Peter Tapp created a proposal to restore the tractor back in 2007.

Four years later, John Deere has completed the restoration project free of charge. The tractor, which Fred Burfield purchased in 1949 to replace the family horse, now looks brand new.

Peggy Burfield, Fred's daughter, got to see the restored tractor in person for the first time June 4 when she rode it in the West Vancouver Community Day parade.

"When they started it, it brought back a flood of memories from my childhood. It sounded just like it did all the time. . . . It was pretty emotional to hear it," she said.

She said when family was told about the restoration project they were very excited.

"History is important to everyone and that's a bit of our family's heritage, so I guess its important to our family's history and the mountain was a huge part of our family," she said.

In 1984, Peggy said her family left the mountain and her father was very disappointed that he had to leave the tractor behind. Peggy said the tractor was their "lifeline." It was used to clear trails and transport necessities, like food and firewood, she said.

Since the Burfields left the mountain more than 25 years ago, the old tractor sat unused and was constantly exposed to the elements until the Tapps, with the support of the Hollyburn Heritage Soceity, decided to revive the rusting machine.

The Tapps have wanted to restore the tractor, more properly called a "crawler" because of its caterpillar tracks, as part of the society's efforts to preserve and protect the history of Hollyburn Mountain since the non-profit society was formed in 1998.

Preserving the mountain's history is personal to the Tapp family. They went up to the mountain to spend time together for years. Bob remembers the sound of the tractor well.

"It's a very distinctive sounding tractor . . . you could hear it across the creek from where our cabin was and we were trying to get the kids to sleep and there was this tractor making all that noise," he said.

Renewing the tractor is one of the many restoration projects the society has taken on since its creation. The society's board of directors wants to use the tractor to draw attention to the society's efforts. They hope to create a pavilion to put pieces of the mountain's heritage, like the tractor, on display.

Peter said the plans to create the pavilion are in the works, but it is going to be a pricey project.

Along with the pavilion museum, he said the society's ultimate goal is to restore Hollyburn Lodge.

Courtesy of the North Shore News

Marion Burfield and her cousin Peggy Burfield standing outside the Burfield Lodge, Sun Peaks, January 27, 2012.

The new Burfield chair lift at Sun Peaks.
Photograph by Marion Burfield

Marion Burfield (left) with her cousin Peggy Burfield and Mayor Al Raine at Tod Mountain's 50 Year Grand Reunion Gala, January 27, 2012.

On January 27, 2012 Sun Peaks Resort hosted a Grand Reunion Gala evening to celebrate 50 years of skiing on Tod Mountain and 20 years as Sun Peaks Resort. In attendance were many old time skiers and their families along with special guests including BC Minister of Environment Terry Lake, Senator Nancy Greene Raine and Mayor of Sun Peaks Al Raine. Also in attendance were Marion Burfield, daughter of the late Harry Burfield, well known on Tod Mountain, and her cousin Peggy Burfield. There were several speeches made by dignitaries along with several personal stories told by long time Tod Mountain skiers. The evening was a great success.

Marion Ann Burfield with her truck, summer of 2010.
Photo by Marion's good friend and co-worker, Steve Tanner.

About the Author

As the second child of Harry and Katherine Burfield, I was born on June 2, 1955 in North Vancouver, British Columbia.

Since Dad came from an English background, one of his favorite stories read to him as a child was *Robin Hood*. My first name came from that story, and Mom gave me her second name.

I spent my first four years at Hollyburn Mountain in West Vancouver. I don't remember much from that era, with the exception of my first experiences of skiing: Dad would strap on our skis and away we would go down the hill. With my tiny skis between his much longer ones, I would hang on to his legs. Dad used the same technique to teach my brother, Richard.

Being a tomboy, I got myself into many predicaments as a child and often found myself injured. At the age of six I broke my leg by the Burfield lodge. The ski patrol didn't have far to go to bring me in. I remember the day when one of George

Winters' horses at White Croft Ranch didn't like what I was feeding him. He turned, kicked me in the face and knocked me out. Richard had to flag down a passer-by to go find our father, who was working on Tod Mountain. Dad eventually rescued me from that field and drove me to the hospital in Kamloops. It was hours before I finally got medical attention in the form of eight stitches on my chin and a few less teeth. That experience didn't stop me from loving horses. Or should I say they loved me? They loved to throw me, pick me up by the scruff of the neck and shake me, bite me and chase me out of their field.

Running was always a favorite sport of mine and it led to one of my childhood nicknames —"Daddy Long Legs." I was three years younger then Rick but always taller than he was until one winter when he came home from the boys' school he attended that year. He was suddenly a great deal taller and I quickly saw that I was in trouble. All the payback was coming. Rick was a jokester like Dad was. We had our brother-sister arguments as many kids do, but they always ended in laughter.

Ten days after my sixteenth birthday, Dad took his last flight. I was going to go with him and his visitors that day, but since Mom had stayed at the store, I decided to help and get dinner ready for everybody. When Mom came home, she sent me to spend the night with a friend. The next day she phoned to ask me to come home. It was then she told me the news.

It is hard to describe one specific feeling in a life turned upside down. Disbelief is a strong one. "This can't happen to us" is another. I remember sitting in the car for hours later that day, maybe because Dad and I had spent so many good times going places and it was always an

Riki Burfield with her son Jaden.

adventure wherever we went. Dad and I often went hunting or fishing together and both our parents kept us busily involved in many sports. Aside from outdoor sports, we also enjoyed many hours playing ping-pong. Dad called it "ganip-ganop". Six years after my father died, the police showed up on my doorstep. They explained that they came to me first with the news of Richard being buried in an avalanche because of what Mom had been through with the death of her husband. They took me to her right away so we could be together. Again we asked "Why is this happening to our family?" Of course, there are never any answers.

For many years I wondered where I belonged, moving around from place to place. For some reason, I always came back to the Kamloops area. I took up a career as a long-haul truck driver, probably for the challenge of getting something that big moving and keeping it going. I have been driving a truck for 25 years now. It isn't the most glamorous job for a woman, but is was a choice that I made. Being a single mom of two kids, I took them with me. It was a strain sometimes, but we managed. Neither of my kids has chosen the job of driving a truck.

I have two outstanding children, both born in Kamloops. My first born, Riki Dawn Burfield, arrived on April 19th, 1979, two years after Rick was killed. She is named after him. My son, Kurt Stacy Burfield, was born on October 12, 1980. Kurt graduated from Kamloops Secondary High School in 1998. He worked locally in Kamloops at a second-hand store. While working

Kurt Burfield with Melissa and their son Joshua.

there he met his life long partner Melissa Dawn Herrett. They now live in Coquitlam, BC and Kurt has taken up a career at a Vancouver printing press. On November 2, 2007 Kurt and Melissa became parents to our first-born grandson Joshua Riley Burfield. Riki now lives just outside of Salmo, BC on her large property in the south Kootenays. Two years ago she gave us the greatest gift, our second grandson, Jaden Quentin Burfield, born in Nelson on Feburary 20, 2010.

Many stories have been lost in the passing of time, but I won't ever forget Dad's love of life and his willingness to share his knowledge with anyone who crossed his path. His love of skiing was very strong, and his dreams were even bigger. In the end, that passion cost him his life. I have no doubt that he would be very honoured to know that his name lives on in a big way at Sun Peaks. My family is also very proud of his contributions. I hope that future generations of the Burfield family will feel the same way.

Writing this book has been emotional at times, bringing back more than forty years of memories. It has also allowed me to do some healing. I hope my wonderful Dad, my loving Mom and my dear brother Richard would be happy to see memories of their lives in book form. It is important for me to offer readers a glimpse of the amazing family I have been a part of.

Dad was known by many as a very colorful character and he was certainly that. He loved and lived life to the fullest. He was one of a kind and I miss him every day. Thanks, Dad, for being in my life, if only for a short sixteen years. You are truly missed—by me and many others.

I hope the readers of this book enjoy what I have spent many years creating as much as I have enjoyed putting it together.

The Burfield Lodge at Sun Peaks.
Photograph by Marion Burfield